GROWING UP WITH YOUR CHILDREN

GROWING UP WITH YOUR CHILDREN

7 Turning Points in the Lives of Parents

Seamus Carey

Rowman & Littlefield Publishers, Inc.
Lanham • Boulder • New York • Toronto • Plymouth, UK

Published by Rowman & Littlefield Publishers, Inc.
A wholly owned subsidiary of
The Rowman & Littlefield Publishing Group, Inc.
4501 Forbes Boulevard, Suite 200, Lanham, Maryland 20706
http://www.rowmanlittlefield.com

Estover Road, Plymouth PL6 7PY, United Kingdom

British Library Cataloguing in Publication Information Available

Library of Congress Cataloging-in-Publication Data

Carey, Seamus, 1965–
  Growing up with your children : 7 turning points in the lives of parents /
Seamus Carey.
      p. cm.
  Includes bibliographical references and index.
  ISBN 978-1-4422-0096-8 (cloth : alk. paper) — ISBN 978-1-4422-0098-2
(electronic)
  1. Parenting—Philosophy. 2. Child rearing—Philosophy. I. Title.
  HQ755.8.C365 2010
  173—dc22   2009024565

Printed in the United States of America

For
Kevin and Ann Marie

Think where man's glory most begins and ends
And say my glory was I had such friends.

—William Butler Yeats

CONTENTS

ACKNOWLEDGMENTS

I am extremely fortunate to work with outstanding colleagues in the Philosophy Department at Manhattan College: Rentaro Hashimoto, David Bollert, Eoin O'Connell, and Alfred DiLascia. Alfred generously took the time to carefully read each chapter of this book and provide invaluable suggestions for improvements. It seems as if I couldn't write books if not for the friendship, encouragement, and editorial eye of Fernand Beck, who read and commented on the entire manuscript as it was being written. I have also benefited from conversations about this book with Jim Mustich and Amelio D'Onofrio. As always, I am most indebted to, and most grateful for, my family: Noreen, Caitriona, Anna, and James. What joy!

INTRODUCTION

Philosophy and Story

Your teenage son is sleeping more than usual lately and he now refuses to get out of bed to meet his teammates for an important game. A few weeks later you remind him of his eleven o'clock curfew as he walks out the door on a Saturday night, but you have to go looking for him as the clock sails past midnight. You find him in a neighborhood bar, and when he mockingly refuses your demand to go home, you become enraged and begin hammering him with your fists until onlookers restrain you. You return home with your dignity as a man and your identity as a father shattered. Over the next few weeks, things spiral downward until your son asks for your help in filling out insurance forms to check into a drug rehabilitation center.

Your nine-year-old daughter has been practicing a piece of music for three months in preparation for a recital at her music school. Each week, after her lesson, the teacher has noted her progress and seems pleased. You've arranged to make the recital a special night for the family, inviting grandparents, relatives, and a couple of friends to the performance, even promising your daughter hot chocolate afterwards. Two nights before the recital, you arrive home from work to an unusually quiet house. It's clear that your daughter has been crying. Your wife summons you to the kitchen to tell you that the music teacher called to say that your daughter isn't ready to perform after all and she will be scheduled for a different recital at a later date.

Over the weekend, you promise your middle-school-age daughter that you will help her study for her final exams when you get home from work on Monday. At the end of the work day, you are tired, but determined to keep your promise. You arrive home and tell your daughter to get her papers ready while you run upstairs to change your clothes. Upon entering the dining room, you find her papers thrown across the table in disorganized piles. After asking some questions to help her organize a study plan, she gets annoyed with you. Your patience is wearing thin, so you tell her to take some time to get her papers and study guides together while you answer some e-mails for work. When you return, she is just as disorganized as she was at the start. You lose your temper and yell at her. She cries and leaves the room. Shortly after, your wife enters to ask what happened. As you explain the situation, your feelings of anger and frustration toward your daughter turn to guilt.

The range of challenges parents face seems to have no limit. Increasing the difficulty for parents in meeting these challenges is the lack of time we have to think and prepare for them. How are parents to respond to trials and traumas such as those mentioned here? Do you punish your son for disobeying rules in order to teach him the value of respecting authority? Do you intervene on behalf of your daughter to protect her from the disappointment of being told her music is not good enough? Do you accept your guilt for yelling at your daughter or try to explain it away? Do we forgive those who let us down? What role, if any, does forgiveness have in everyday family life?

These questions are difficult to answer. But these are the kinds of questions that philosophers have been asking and responding to for more than two thousand years. Philosophy has been cultivated by the world's greatest thinkers, who have devoted themselves to studying the human condition, its potential and its limitations, its ways of knowing and its sources of strength. It is a hidden treasure of wisdom waiting to be uncovered that can help us parent with greater insight and conviction. The philosophical corpus contains a profound understanding of human beings and human relationships, as well as the best strategies for making wise decisions and for living a good life.

Yet, curiously, philosophers have remained almost silent on the issues of family and parenting. And while there are ample resources within the literature that can benefit parents and families, the language and writing styles of philosophers tend to obfuscate their intent and their relevance to everyday, working parents. As a result, parents have been deprived of wisdom that can guide them as they navigate the treacherous waters of child rearing while seeking to find personal fulfillment in their own lives. *Growing Up with Your Children: 7 Turning Points in the Lives of Parents* will begin to reverse this deficiency in the philosophical literature and in doing so introduce parents to the deepest wisdom we have for dealing with the challenges of family life.

At first glance, the turn to philosophy is not obvious or easy because parents have been saturated with psychological approaches to problem solving within the family. If we seek out assistance in dealing with family issues, we are usually directed to some form of psychologist or psychiatrist. These fields are useful to many, but not all. Dominated by practitioners who see human beings through the mechanistic lens of science, medicine, and the diagnoses of mental illness, these professions provide only a limited account of what is possible and healthy in the realm of parenting. This is one reason for the explosion of people being diagnosed as pathological and for the shameful amount of psychotropic medicine being dispersed to the American public, especially children. The pharmaceutical industry is profiting from a narrowing conception of normal human behavior and human development that is based on largely unexamined assumptions of what it means to be a healthy person, but parents and children are not.

In contrast, philosophers have, from the beginning, recognized that perfectly healthy individuals can benefit from philosophical dialogue and insight, not only to overcome specific problems, but to live a better life. Unfortunately, because philosophy has become so specialized, it is almost entirely inaccessible to the average person. It hasn't always been this way. Originally, philosophy was an activity that benefited ordinary people. As the Stoic philosopher Epicurus points out, a philosophical argument that does not cure any ailment is empty.

Before Epicurus, Socrates devoted his life to philosophy, which he did primarily in the public square. In doing so, Socrates saw himself as a servant of the people, and the service he was providing them was to wake people up to what was most important in their lives—caring for their own souls. In his view, nothing was more important. In talking with the people of Athens, he forced them to examine how they were living. In the process, Socrates exposed flaws in their thinking and a dissonance between their ideals and their habits of acting. By asking the right questions and exposing inconsistencies in their lives, he was helping the people of Athens to live better lives. For Socrates, this is the primary role of philosophy—a service to help people uncover and remove or overcome obstacles to living better lives.

What could be more valuable to parents? While most of the psychological literature aimed at parents tells them how to better care for their children, few make a point of helping parents care for themselves. They discuss how children grow and assume that parents are finished growing. But parents also grow and develop while meeting the responsibilities of guiding children toward the best life possible. If we direct all of our attention to the development of children, personal development and fulfillment is likely to elude the parent. As we all know, we are not at our best in caring for others when we feel unfulfilled ourselves. Negative emotions and feelings combined with illogical or confused thoughts creep into our relationships if we do not experience fulfillment, or at least the hope for it. Feeling frustrated, we yell at a child when a simple question might have cleared the air. Out of resentment, we gossip about a neighbor, setting a poor model for children to follow, when a different perspective might uncover the neighbor's strengths.

Our children are defenseless against our negative emotions and feelings, which are often unconsciously and unpredictably directed at them. Under these circumstances, no formulaic method, technique, or mental diagnosis will enable us to adequately care for our children. The only antidote to these corrosive emotions is to turn them around, to recover and tap into our own life-affirming wisdom and strength, by transforming negative emotions or confused thoughts into positive and clear ones. To turn from the negative to the positive, from control to acceptance, from vengeance to forgiveness, from narrow individualism to community, from selfishness to gratitude, from guilt to responsibility, and from conformity to faith is to unleash a power unlike any other. The philosophical turning points this book addresses, and the inner strength they reveal, will not only make good parenting possible, but also fulfilling.

STORY

Contemporary Irish philosopher Richard Kearney claims that "telling stories is as basic to human beings as eating. More so, in fact, for while food makes us live, stories are what make our lives worth living. They are what make our condition *human.*"[1] Stories change the world, sometimes literally, as evidenced by the power of a shamanic story that Kearney recalls in which a woman, who was on the verge of death during a difficult childbirth, is somehow saved. "Suffering from a blocked womb, she is told the myth of the 'good' warriors freeing a prisoner trapped in a cave by monsters, and on hearing the plot resolution recited by the shaman, she gives birth to her child."[2]

Not all stories have the power to transform a woman's physiology and save her life during childbirth. Nonetheless, it is true that we cannot live without stories. Less dramatic stories transform our lives in smaller ways by opening up new perspectives on the world and ourselves. To see one's life in a new story, from a different point of view, is liberating. Like the man who cannot find his glasses because he is wearing them, we often forget that the point of view from which we see the world is but one among many. Stories loosen the chains of our all-too-familiar points of view. Alternative perspectives indicate new possibilities, new ways of doing familiar tasks. A new way may be more efficient, or it may just simply be different. But because it is new, it adds to the color of life. Through stories we find these new perspectives, new colors, and alternative ways to relate with and care for children.

Put another way, stories give life meaning. Since the beginning of Western civilization, we have relied on stories to learn our place in the world. It is through stories that we come to know what is expected of us and what we expect of ourselves. When somebody asks us who we are, we tell them our story. In telling our story, we must decide what to include and what to leave out. These decisions, if we are to pay attention to them, tell us a great deal about what we think of ourselves, that is, who we think we are and what we value about our past and our future. In telling our stories, we remember things about ourselves that had been long forgotten. In projecting a future and what we aspire to, we reveal what we value most, where we want to go, what we want to achieve.

Given the central role of story in making sense of our days and lives, *Growing Up with Your Children* relies on stories from the lives of parents and families to illuminate turning points that we go through in the process of raising children and becoming more fulfilled adults. Some stories are based on local events and people, while others recount widely circulated stories with which most readers will be familiar. Whether local or global, each story presents a turning point that is emblematic of issues that are universal to parents.

By themselves, these stories will benefit parents in several important ways. To know that other parents have faced circumstances similar to our own makes us realize that we are not alone. To know we are not alone is reassuring, perhaps even comforting, especially in difficult circumstances. To see how other parents respond to difficult situations enables us to evaluate how we have responded or would respond in similar circumstances. Moreover, to see heroic responses of other parents helps us to realize that we, too, are capable of more than we can imagine. This awareness can propel us to attempt things we might otherwise not consider.

ABOUT STORIES

As valuable as it is to hear or read stories that are relevant to our lives, their impact is magnified when we understand some of the dynamics that operate beneath their surface. Drawing upon the world's greatest thinkers, past and present, *Growing Up with Your Children* turns a philosophical gaze on stories and characters to reveal their inner dynamics and make them more relevant and useful to parents. By using philosophy to clarify some of the hidden insight of stories and their characters, we will be better able to avoid the pitfalls that often hinder parents and to pursue what is most expedient.

An important theme that emerges from our philosophical reading of stories is that changing the course of our parenting journey begins with changing ourselves. Not that we shouldn't work for change outside the family when we see problems or injustices in the world. But the most important and lasting changes that parents need to be concerned with are those that we actually have some control over. Philosophy encourages us to turn our attention inward, to examine our habits of thinking and acting, and to see how our habits coincide with or differ from the ideals we aspire to live by. When we turn our attention inward, there are two important insights that usually emerge. First, we rarely live up to the ideals we espouse, and second, we have accumulated much more insight and wisdom than we realize. By bringing these two realizations to the fore, we can close the gap between our habits and our ideals by relying on our own inherent wisdom and insight. Philosophy, then, is most effective for parents as a process of remembering or recovery.

In the midst of our busy lives, we consciously process only a fraction of what we experience. The experiences that are not processed by consciousness, however, do not simply disappear. They are tucked away in the hidden caverns of consciousness. From these hidden depths, they continue to shape our perceptions, attitudes, and emotions toward the world. While hidden, however, we have little control over how they affect us. As a process of remembering, philosophy helps us to bring their hidden content into the light of day so that we can have a say in how those experiences affect us and our views of the world. Philosophy, then, can be thought of, in part, as a process of recovering forgotten dimensions of ourselves.

Thought of in this way, philosophy is not pretending to teach much that is new. Its goal is to help parents to better understand and use resources we already have in order to parent more effectively and to live more fully. In other words, philosophy begins with the presupposition that we already have the insight and wisdom we need; we just have to learn how to retrieve it from beneath layers of false ideas, flawed arguments, and wayward expectations. To find the wisdom and insight we need to parent well, we must move through turning points that lead inward.

TURNING POINTS

In interviews with parents for this book, I received many different responses when I asked parents about the most significant turning points in their lives as parents. If I addressed all of them, this book would be far too long. I settled on the seven included in this volume because they most effectively capture both goals of the book—more insightful parenting and more fulfilled parents. The turning points that are presented in these stories are emblematic, not only of the difficult issues parents deal with each day, but also of the type of changes we would like to accomplish. Once parents get beyond the basics of how to feed, hold, and dress a child, our job requires thought. At each turn there are decisions to be made, and if we do not take hold of these decisions as thoughtful parents, they are made for us, often in ways that we do not want. Prior to working through these turning points, we find familiar ways in which life is controlling parents instead of parents controlling their lives. In order to reverse this relationship we must turn our attention inward to examine where we are, how we got there, and where we want to go.

There is symmetry to the book's structure. The themes of the first three chapters deal with universal challenges parents face in their relationships with children, while the last three chapters deal with virtues that benefit parents in guiding children and in finding personal fulfillment. In between these two sections is a chapter dealing with community, a central turning point that all parents must negotiate and the site in which all other turning points occur.

The first chapter, which deals with parental power, tells a familiar but tragic tale of a father's misunderstanding of his authority. His attempt to transfer the strength that served him so well in most areas of his life caused painful conflict with his son. Once this division took root, he was unable to turn it around until he and his son came to blows, literally. By that point, his son had become an alcoholic and needed help. In response to his son's plea, his father underwent a major turning point in his life and understood that his real power as a father is not found in authoritarianism and physical strength, but in support and understanding. This turn leads us to reflect on the nature of power and its role in the lives of parents. Parental power and authority is real and cannot be ignored, so we need to understand it. If we fail to understand it, we are likely to use it in unwise and hurtful ways.

The second chapter addresses an increasingly problematic area for parents and all those who work with children: parental advocacy. Knowing when and how to advocate for our children is a challenge as they become involved with increasing numbers of teachers, coaches, and counselors. This chapter presents examples of necessary advocacy, inappropriate advocacy, and the absence of advocacy. There are some instances in which parents have an obligation to advocate on behalf of their children. When there is systemic or individual injustice, it is appropriate for parents to stand up for their children. Unfortunately, parents are increasingly engaging in inappropriate advocacy. More and more we hear stories of parents fighting for their son or daughter to play on a sports team or defending their child against the disciplinary measures levied by a school for misbehavior. These stories demonstrate that parents do not always serve their children well by advocating for them. The final story of the chapter is an example of when it is appropriate to simply let a child's disappointment stand. Sometimes by working through disappointment, children and their parents can learn important life lessons.

Guilt is one of the most common and troublesome experiences parents have in dealing with their children. In the third chapter, we meet Will Bookman, who finds himself burdened by the weight of guilt after losing his patience with his adolescent daughter. Tired from a long day at work, he agrees to uphold his commitment to study with his daughter when he arrives home. His daughter, however, is woefully unprepared and seemingly disinterested. After patiently trying to help her to organize her materials and receiving no effort in return, he finds himself yelling at his daughter. She cries, and he feels guilty. Bookman's response to this guilt is enlightening for all parents who face the inevitable discomfort and burden of guilt.

While we work to minimize actions that lead to guilt, we also recognize that we are never guilt-free. This is not because we are always doing things that are wrong. It is because, at any given moment, we have many possibilities, but we can only choose one of them. The others go unfulfilled and leave us feeling empty, incomplete, or, as twentieth-century

German philosopher Martin Heidegger describes it, guilty. This guilt is not a direct response to a specific act. It is more persistent, embedded in the core of what it is to be human. Recognizing this embedded sense of guilt leads us to take our choices, and hence our lives, more seriously. As a result, it is an important first step in avoiding choices that lead to the more transitory experiences of guilt. And for some, it can lead to a more mature life in which we take greater responsibility for our actions. In doing so, we become more authentic individuals.

Chapter 4, at the center of the text, deals with community. Community is at the center because it is not only a turning point that parents must constantly negotiate; it is also the turning point in which the six other turning points unfold. As a turning point, community takes us from the myth of self that pervades the American psyche to the self that is dialogical and communal down to its very core. As much as we admire and idealize the self-made man or woman, the reality is that we are never completely independent from the communities in which we live. Even the most successful and dynamic individuals rely on others, on laws, on people from the past, on ideals for the future in order to achieve their goals. We are inescapably embedded in communities and for parents to understand this reality is a first step toward finding a clearer understanding about how to negotiate community, to set realistic goals, and to find some peace of mind.

One of the more subtle and most easily overlooked turning points is the one in which we move from selfishness and self-centeredness to gratitude. Chapter 5 presents stories of the transformative power of gratitude as well as the challenges of dealing with the inevitable lack of gratitude in children. This lack makes it difficult for both children and parents to cultivate the virtue of gratitude. But there are unique benefits that come with gratitude, which the Roman statesman Cicero describes as "the parent of all virtues."

Since gratitude is a virtue that is oriented toward the past, toward what has already occurred or what one has already received, it is critically important that we never give up on our past. The past shapes our view of the present and our orientation toward the future. The past is central to our personal stories or narratives. These narratives determine the meaning of our lives. They tell us how we understand ourselves, what we are, what we want to be, what we value, and what we don't. If these narratives do not have a place for gratitude, our lives are diminished. If we are to find gratitude, and the benefits that come with it, we need to be vigilantly open to our past, to allow old events to have new meaning in light of the present. The parent that can cultivate gratitude will not only be more effective in guiding her children, but will be more joyful in doing so.

Forgiveness is, perhaps, the most difficult, emotionally charged turning point of all. Many disagree about what forgiveness is, when it is appropriate, or whether it is ever appropriate. For instance, philosopher Vladimir Jankelevitch describes forgiveness as an ineffable, spontaneous act of freedom, a miracle. As a result, he argues that nothing is unforgivable. French philosopher Jacques Derrida, widely known as the founder of deconstructionism, suggests that some things may be impossible to forgive; yet remaining open to the possibility of forgiving what may be impossible to forgive is an ideal that can keep the human heart from turning cold. Seventeenth-century philosopher Baruch Spinoza sees rational understanding as a balm that can alleviate the most painful emotions, turning the negativity of hate and vengeance into love and bypassing the need for forgiveness altogether.

Despite the differences among philosophers about forgiveness, what it is, how it is achieved, and when it is appropriate, they all agree that those who forgive liberate themselves from the pain and suffering that endure beyond the initial transgression. They are careful to delineate the differences between justice and forgiveness, so that achieving one does not eliminate the other. I can forgive someone while insisting that he receives justice.

Parents regularly face the challenge to forgive. Sometimes we must decide whether or not to forgive someone who has hurt our child. Sometimes we are forced to forgive our own children, and sometimes we must ask our children for forgiveness for our own transgressions. None of these are easy. In chapter 6, not only will we encounter stubborn obstacles to forgiveness, but we will also see how forgiveness can alleviate debilitating grudges and tensions in everyday family life.

While commentary on parenting and family life has been dominated by psychology, conversations about faith are almost universally thought to be religious. And yet the mother who cares for her sick child or resists bringing unhealthy snacks to children's sporting events just to fit in, or the father who takes a new job to improve the lives of his family relies on faith also. But the faith that we rely on in our everyday lives is not, primarily, religious faith. There is a secular or philosophical faith at the core of everything we do, great or small, that functions like a sixth sense for those who are aware of it and trust in it. This faith enables us to identify principles that are in line with the type of people we want to be, and it gives us the courage to live in accordance with them, even when the trends of society are against us. Philosophical faith, which includes faith in oneself, faith in the world, and faith in children, allows us to see and to pursue alternatives to how we live rather than accepting unsatisfactory circumstances as fate.

Philosophical faith is not something that we can create or implant in people, nor do we need to. We already have philosophical faith, and we use it all the time. It is often obscured, however, by the pace and the demands of everyday life, especially family life. Heightening our awareness of this faith is empowering. In chapter 7, we consider stories that show how this faith is eroding before our eyes, as well as stories that demonstrate its power.

Despite the power of stories and philosophical insight, few can doubt the difficulty of changing patterns of parenting behavior. One need only look at the amount of books lining the shelves of bookstores offering advice on how to do it better. "Experts" churn out page upon page of strategies and methods on everything from how to talk to our children to how to get them into college. At the same time, extracurricular activities for children are popping up like chicken-pox spots on a child's skin. As more and more opportunities arise for children to join an activity or a team, we find it hard to resist out of fear that our child will fall behind if she doesn't participate. Parents have even taken to holding children back from school for a year so they can get an edge up on their peers, who have come to be regarded, primarily, as competition.

This hyper-competitive style of parenting is one example of parents losing their way and abandoning the wisdom they already have to parent well. This forgetfulness is destructive to children and parents alike. It is destructive to children because it robs them of the time they need to be creative, to engage in free play, and to simply be quiet and bored. It is out of moments of quiet and boredom that creativity is born and during free play that they learn how to organize their thoughts and relationships with each other, to negotiate differences and agree on self-determining rules. By overscheduling their days, we prevent them from learning who they are and most want to be. Instead, we force upon them an idea of who we want them to be. To make matters worse, the ideas of who we want them to be are rarely our own. These ideas come from prevailing social trends often adopted by parents with little thought or reflection. As a result, parents are frenetically driving children from one place to the next, losing themselves and their family life in activities that are benefitting nobody except those getting paid to provide them.

While most of the literature aimed at parents focuses on the children, it is the parents that need to make the adjustments if we are to reverse destructive trends. This is hard work, but for parents and their children there is nothing more important. Philosophy has the resources to show us the way not only to direct us from our shortcomings, but also to show us the way toward real fulfillment and joy.

To strive for fulfillment and joy might seem a little naïve to parents who are burdened with the anxiety of mounting debt, drinking teenagers, and crying babies. But the joy we aspire to as a result of working through difficult turning points is not the empty, fleeting joy that accompanies futile attempts to escape our burdens. The philosophical approach to working through the critical turning points of parenting understands that tensions do not go away when we solve a problem. Tensions merely shift from one event and one moment to the next. The joy we aspire to embraces the tensions of life. With philosophical insight, we engage the right tensions and avoid the wrong ones. When chosen with insight, the tensions in which we engage reveal what is best in human nature. Supported by the wisdom, insight, and courage of philosophy, parents don't want to turn away from the difficulties of life because we know that we can achieve blessedness and sublimity by working though them.

1

POWER

I recently attended the funeral of one of my favorite people, Jim Healy. He was a family friend and visited our house on Saturday nights for many years along with a group of five or six other Irishmen. They talked for hours, mostly about Irish football and hurling. Jim was a native Irish speaker and his proud and powerful voice grew deeper and stronger when a fellow Irish speaker showed up, as they did from time to time. Jim's Irish was the best, they said. He won Irish speaking competitions when he was a youngster growing up in West Kerry.

Like so many of his generation, poverty forced Jim away from home. He went to England first and then New York, working hard on construction sites. He eventually found a steady job cleaning a food plant outside New York City. One night during a blizzard, the bus that he rode to work stopped running five or six miles away from his stop. He hopped off with the other passengers and when they turned back, he continued on foot, all the way to work. When he arrived, everyone had gone home and the drab building seemed even grayer than usual. He settled into his shift, moving from room to room, scrubbing, cleaning, organizing things that had been left out and putting them in their place. As he was finishing up in one of the offices, he noticed an unusual bag on the floor. He opened it to find rolls of money. The guards who transported the money in armored cars were trying to beat the bad weather and inadvertently left it behind.

Jim immediately secured it away in his locker, finished his rounds, and walked home in the wind and snow. Then next day, he arrived at work an hour early and brought the bag straight to the manager's office. He told him where and when he found it. The manger thanked him. Jim later learned that there was $50,000 in the bag and laughed with his friends, who teased him for not taking the money, something he was never tempted to do. The determination that got him to work that evening and the honesty that brought him in early the next day ensured that the necessities of life would be provided for himself and for his family, which eventually grew to include four children.

The church was full for his funeral. There was a deep and secure silence throughout the mass that felt like a womb for the Irish that the young priest shared in song at the Eucharistic prayer. The phonetic rhythm of the Irish language evoked a sense of privacy and privilege, its ancient soul somehow bringing everyone closer to the divine. Whispering voices sporadically flittered in the air like incense above the congregants praying and singing note for note with the priest. Some of those voices were early middle-aged women, but most were Jim Healy's friends: Andy Purcell, Jim Brosnan, Mickey Donnelly, Tim Doheny, and many others, including my father. Most of these men never got accustomed to wearing suits and ties, their white heads never perfectly neat. These are proud, intelligent, and strong men who prospered in America after having cultivated stomach muscles over pick and spade as children, muscles that never left them. These muscles have grown tame with time, but this day they were called upon once more, working from memory more than strength, convulsed with pride to hold back tears for their friend, who they consulted for Irish words and sayings, for a hand at the cement and at the wheelbarrow.

Jim's oldest son, Sean, gave the eulogy. He opened by reiterating what was obvious to those who knew Jim; he was a man of great faith. Sean carried that thought a step further with humor by adding, "And I tested it often." He continued, confessing, "I was a wise guy, ya know," and this became a refrain throughout the eulogy as he fumbled and pushed forward with words to finally say what he intended.

Sean is my age. We grew up together, though we weren't always closest friends. We went to the same schools and we were teammates on the local Irish football team. Sean was average height, but powerful, his dense body mass adding to his strength. He played in the backs as a defender on our team. Although he lacked speed, his strength made him very effective. He managed to move people where he wanted to move them, and when he could get momentum going forward with the ball, he would always deliver it to the forwards. We had a good team. We won most of our games, and every second year, at age ten, twelve, and fourteen, when we were the oldest players in our division, we won the championship. That streak ended at the age of sixteen though. We didn't win the under-eighteen championship.

Things began to change in our small community when we became teenagers, reaching a tipping point somewhere in our late teens, when the hinges of family life began to come undone. The primary reason was alcohol. We all began drinking too young. Some of us managed to turn back from the ravages of alcohol through sports, parental fear, or love. Some went painfully far before turning around. And some never turned at all.

Sean's alcoholic slide became all too clear to me on an early spring Sunday morning. The sun felt a little too bright and the breeze still carried a chill that made it too cold to play Irish football. Most of us had lost our enthusiasm for the game by now. Some of our teammates were heading off to Ivy League colleges, on their way to distinguished careers in medicine, law, and finance. Others were primarily interested in how they looked and the girls they might attract. Still others couldn't or wouldn't look past the weekend, when they would drink cases and kegs in the park. Being awakened early on a cool Sunday morning to play a game in Gaelic Park, a field that was more sand and dust than grass, was an unwelcome burden to most of us. It was so unappealing on this particular day that we were struggling to round up enough players to field a team.

Jim Healy and my father were good friends. Whenever there was work to be done, they helped each other. My father was a skilled carpenter and builder. He worked in the carpenter's union during the day and worked for himself building houses in the evenings and on the weekends. Whenever he had a job, Jim Healy helped. His unabashed enthusiasm for work was contagious. Whether we were mixing cement, demolishing old houses, or painting, he dove into the job with the joy of a child jumping into puddles on a walk home from school. His gait behind a wheelbarrow full of cement was determined and direct, almost light, in sharp contrast to the weight of the load he was pushing. He wasn't a leader or an organizer. He wanted his role to be defined clearly, and his favorite role was collecting cement in a wheelbarrow from the end of a chute at the back of a cement truck, driving it across a muddy building sight, and heaving it into a filling form with the stiff power of his short and muscular arms and legs. And at the end of a hard day, after scrubbing shovels, rakes, trowels, and wheelbarrows to a shine, he liked to linger beside them, leaning on the handle of a shovel for a few minutes in a tired but buoyant stance, satisfied, before sliding out of his rubber boots and walking home.

He was up early on Sunday, and his neighborly greetings resounded through streets and open windows as he made his way to and from seven o'clock Mass. He rarely stopped into our house on Sunday mornings, so it was unusual when I heard him in the kitchen while I packed my Irish football gear into a bag. The voices were lower than usual, and then I heard my father coming toward my room. He leaned inside the door and asked, "Will you come over to Jim's house and get Sean to go to the game?" I knew I had no choice, but I made a faint effort to get out of it by saying that the game didn't matter much anyway. In part, I was reluctant because Sean and I had grown apart over the past couple of years.

The last few times I was with him, I watched in amazement as he walked up to the park benches beside the tennis courts in Indian Field just after dark on a Friday or Saturday night with his light-blue high school football jacket, embroidered with large yellow letters across the back, announcing his team. His right arm was elevated in the shape of a backwards C, wrapped around a case of Budweiser nips resting on his shoulder. On colder nights, there would be a fire in a metal garbage can to keep us warm while the air kept the beer cold. When the weather warmed, the bottles rested between layers of crushed ice in garbage cans swiped from driveways along the route from the beer distributor to the park. His case of beer, however, was not for sharing. Sean had built a tolerance for alcohol consumption that was hard to comprehend, even for those of us who witnessed it. Most nights, he would not leave the park until he had finished every beer, all twenty-four of them. I didn't know if that was what he had done on this particular weekend, but I was pretty sure the reason he wasn't getting out of bed was related, and I also knew that his bedroom was not going to be a welcoming place.

I walked the two short blocks to his house in silence next to my father and Jim Healy. On the one hand, I felt grown up in being asked to do something for them. On the other hand, I felt as if I were about to enter enemy territory as a traitor working for the other side. "He's in there," Jim said, pointing to his bedroom door. It was close to 10:30 in the morning, but the small room was dark, the shades pulled completely across the only window in the room. I walked in and closed the door. The absence of the stale stench of alcohol that follows a night of heavy boozing surprised me and gave me a flicker of hope. Maybe he wasn't hung over with a headache and the self-loathing that drinking brings to its abusers. Maybe all he needs is a little encouragement from a teammate to become interested in the game. But these thoughts were sharply interrupted when he rolled over on his pillow and said, "What are you doing here?" "Your dad asked me to talk to you to see if you would get up and come play the game. I know the game doesn't mean that much. I don't feel like playing myself. But it's a nice day and getting a little run in will give you the rest of the day," I said. "Na. I'm not going," he replied.

I expected his response, and a part of me wanted to leave then and there, while another part of me thought ahead to the two powerful Irishmen waiting outside, hoping for results. "C'mon, Sean. It's just an hour. We need ya." "I'm not going today," he responded, his words becoming shorter and more direct with a trace of irritation. "Sean, your father and my father are standing outside waiting for us. Just throw on a pair of pants and grab your cleats. You can get some sleep when we get back." "Get the fuck out of my room, before I kick your fuckin' ass," he snarled, and there was no doubt that he meant it. He might not have smelled like stale booze, but he wasn't any more pleasant for it. He was not coming to the game for me or anyone else.

At this point I was embarrassed to be in his space. The room felt smaller than when I entered. And yet I moved only reluctantly to the door because I knew I now had to face my father and, worse still, his. As I closed the door behind me, I saw my father standing alone at the front door. I walked sheepishly toward him, not sure how he would respond. "Is he coming?" he asked. "No," I said. I looked through the glass of the front door and saw Jim Healy waiting anxiously on the sunlit sidewalk. My father began to ask me if I would try once more but I cut him off before I would have to give him the details of what was said and told him, "There's no way he's coming." He knew I had tried my best, but he was disappointed for his friend. I walked out first. Jim Healy's eyes were glued to the door and then me, wide in nervous anticipation. I walked down the four steps of his stoop, and he knew by the look on my face that his son was staying in bed.

Changes that were long underway became clearly defined that morning. And as the expression on Jim Healy's face turned from possibility to defeat, he had undergone a decisive turning point in his life as a father. Any semblance of authority and direct influence over his son was gone. His directives meant nothing to Sean anymore. In fact, Sean's anger and resentment only heightened his defiance. Something else was driving Sean's life, and the strains of their relationship had filtered outside their private battleground of a home. As much as Sean wanted his Sunday-morning darkness and his toxic defiance of his father to remain private, cooped up inside his aggravated space, my father and I were the awkward witnesses to a fractured relationship. He was deep into a downward spiral that was being accelerated with booze and worse.

Sean wouldn't find his way out of his downward spiral before accentuating the schism from his father a couple of weeks later outside a bar around the corner from his house. Trying to hold onto his authority in the house, Jim Healy told Sean to be home by eleven o'clock as he was leaving the house on a Saturday night. Jim suspected he might not be listening and so watched where he went, which was to a local bar, one of the twenty-six that dotted the streets of our neighborhood that spanned all of one square mile. Jim let him stay until it passed eleven o'clock and waited outside until he saw someone he knew come from the bar. Paul McCaffrey emerged with a group of friends, and Jim asked him if he would go back in to tell Sean to come outside. Almost all of the teenagers and young adults in our neighborhood had the highest respect for other people's parents in the neighborhood, especially proud and hardworking ones like Jim Healy. Paul went straight back into the bar to deliver the message to Sean. He had been drinking for several hours and, over the years, his substance use had graduated from just beer to include whiskey and, more recently, cocaine.

Upon hearing his father was outside, Sean resolved to defy him by not going out. But the patrons at the bar, his friends and others who hardly knew him, wouldn't let him stay without going outside to see what his father wanted. Succumbing to their pressure, he walked outside, temporarily concealing the rage he brought with him. His father grabbed Sean by the arm and told him that he was coming home with him. Sean swung his arm away from his father and told him to keep his hands off him. By this time, a few patrons had gathered around and Jim Healy was now enraged. He struck a powerful blow with his fist into Sean's arm. Insulated by the numbing effect of alcohol, Sean made a defiant stance, turning to his father, gesturing with the wave of his hand as if to shoo away a fly, saying, "Mosquitoes, Dad, mosquitoes." Sean's health and their relationship, both hanging by a thread that night, were saved from irreparable damage by the surrounding patrons as they held Jim Healy back from his son. They managed to keep him away until he was calm enough to walk home, which he did, alone.

I didn't see Jim Healy for several weeks after this incident until he came into my parent's house during lunch on an early summer afternoon. He had called moments earlier to see if my mother was home because he needed her help with insurance forms. Sean had been working in the carpenter's union for more than a year and had excellent medical benefits, although getting the proper coverage for alcohol and drug rehabilitation required extra paperwork with which Jim Healy needed assistance. He entered our house as he always did, with a quick step and excitable voice. He held out his papers as he approached my mother and explained that they were for Sean to get help. His distress was tempered with relief as he repeatedly invoked God's help to make the turn that Sean needed in his life.

"I can't believe it has come to this," he said in dismay, but quickly countered with the prayerful tone of his Irish dialect, "Please God, this will be the help he needs." My mother filled out as many of the forms as she could and showed Jim what he needed to do with the remainder. A woman of equal faith, she reassured Jim Healy over a cup of tea that if he was drinking too much, medical help was the best thing for Sean. He was drinking too much, and I realized that I didn't smell booze in his room when I went to ask him to play Irish football because he was already using cocaine. But Jim's presence in my parent's house that afternoon indicated that Sean had hit some kind of bottom, since he was willing to get help that included a role for his father.

Sean was struggling to contain his emotions as he moved toward the end of his eulogy, but he was no longer struggling with the demons that threatened to undo his life. He stood at the pulpit of the old parish church a sober man with a family of his own, not having had a drink in more than twenty years. His eulogy had several salient messages, one being that he wasn't the best son; he was a "wise guy." But he had come to realize what his father had done for him and that he was now a better person and a better father for having been around his father. He concluded with a message addressed directly to his father, with a church full of Jim Healy's friends as witnesses: "The thing that you wanted most for us, that we would be alright and take care of ourselves, has come to pass. We're okay, Dad. We can all fend for ourselves because of you. Thank you." All of Jim Healy's faithful friends knew that Jim surely was okay, too. He always returned what wasn't his, and an honest life makes for a peaceful rest. This knowledge was his enduring gift to his family and friends.

THE PARADOX OF POWER

The steel will of immigrants like Jim Healy, who came to this country to make a living, was an asset in almost every area of life. Jim's strength enabled him to overcome obstacles that many of weaker constitution could not. This strength combined brute physical force with a fierce determination to see things through to the end. Strength and determination are widely admired traits, largely because those who have them are most productive. They exert power over their circumstances and manage to express their will with force and creativity.

The mere ability to express one's power, however, does not always lead to desired outcomes. Power is often misused on many different levels from the political to the personal. Sometimes those with power misuse it intentionally, seeking to gain a self-interested advantage over the weak or vulnerable. Other times, the misuse of power is unintentional. Either way, the misuse of power usually leaves destruction and hurt in its wake.

Jim Healy had noble intentions as a father, and he did not intentionally misuse his power. Like so many parents, he simply did not understand the nature of his power, how to best use it, or the consequences of misusing it. Nor did he have the time or the inclination to refine the strength of his will and body to adequately meet his son's needs. His approach to parenting, unfortunately, was similar to the approach he took in demolishing a house, which we did one Saturday, along with several neighbors.

I was on the roof, removing the sheathing piece by piece, sliding it over the edge and letting it fall to the ground. Others were working on the floor below, removing plaster walls and flooring. Upon seeing the stud-framing revealed from behind the walls, Jim Healy got excited by the possibility of knocking out the studs with a sledge hammer. He forgot that the studs were supporting the roof and those of us on top of it. With ferocious swings of the sledge, the steel head hit the wood studs, giving off a deep thud. The house shook with each blow. Several men had to yell at the top of their deep voices to get Jim to stop before we all came down on top of him.

As Jim Healy moved away from his childhood on the west coast of Ireland and waded into the world, his strength and determination enabled him to overcome most of life's challenges. But just as in knocking down a house, power can be devastatingly destructive if it is delivered in the wrong way, at the wrong time, or in the wrong place. The benefits of power are rarely as obvious as they might seem. In fact, it is often the use of power that diminishes it. This is the first paradox of power and a good reason for parents to gain an understanding of the nature of power.

POWER IN RELATIONSHIPS

To have power over someone or something is to be in a relationship. There is no master without a slave and no slave without a master. They depend on each other to be who they are. Out of fear of punishment and pain, a slave stays in the relationship and thereby grants power to the master. The slave could choose to take that power away by leaving, even if leaving means dying. Put another way, once the slave is motivated by something other than his fear of being punished and decides to end the relationship, he can, in which case the master no longer has power over him.

Ralph Waldo Emerson, the first American philosopher to gain international renown, offers a variation on the ways in which power is drained from the powerful when he observes, "Infancy conforms to nobody; all conform to it; so that one babe commonly makes four or five of the adults who prattle and play to it."[1] The most vulnerable, Emerson shows, can be the most alluring to those who overwhelm them with knowledge and power. Perhaps it is because the infant has nothing to fear, or because she has what the adult lacks, a simple kind of wholeness. The infant's mind is unburdened by the concerns and calculations of adulthood, the give and take of practical affairs, and the tactics of retaining power. In their nonconforming simplicity, infants, with no effort, make us, the more powerful, conform to them. We find their dependent state of helplessness irresistible and dote over their every gesture and sound.

But that is only part of the story. Parents don't just prattle, we also punish. We guide and goad, coax and coach, discipline and demand. We use our power and authority to insist that our children conform to various practices and procedures. We have to. Children need this knowledge in order to survive in the world. It is through the customs and values that we demonstrate and demand of them, that they become a part of the human family. But just as with an effective demolition job, it can be hard to know when to swing the sledge and when to simply pull a nail. Do I administer harsh punishment to my son the first time he comes home with alcohol on his breath to make him regret what he did and hope he won't want to suffer the same consequences again? Or do I try to talk to him calmly and help him to understand the emotions that lead to using alcohol as an escape? These are difficult choices that parents are faced with regularly, and, unlike Jim Healy on the demolition job, parents usually don't have other adults around with answers that can save us.

It is difficult to be the son of a man who relies heavily on his power, and it can be difficult for such a man to be a good father. Jim Healy thought he could control his offspring the way he controlled the rest of his life. He tried to parent with the same approach he used to build, demolish, and walk through blizzards in the snow. This strength and willfulness gave him control over his son only for a while and forced the boy's emerging spirit to remain quiet for too long. His authoritarian approach failed to acknowledge and affirm his son's emotional development and his need for increasing independence. Instead, Jim's willfulness unfairly challenged the lesser strength of his son. Stifled for too long, his son's frustrated spirit roared in ways father and son wished it hadn't, and led Sean down the crooked and painful path of substance abuse. The temporary, if illusory, sense of freedom that alcohol gave Sean was, perhaps, his way of compensating for the lack of power he felt in his relationship with his father.

POWER IN THE SELF

As all parents know, or quickly come to learn, the human spirit is hard to keep down. Children have their own emerging power, what Spinoza calls the *conatus*. This is the innate drive for self-preservation and fulfillment that propels each living being forward into the world. In fact, in his classic work, called *The Ethics*, Spinoza argues that this power is the primary virtue. All other virtues, he argues, depend on power. There is no forgiveness or charity or justice without the power of the *conatus*, or the will for self-preservation and self-realization.[2]

The power Spinoza has in mind is different from the power on which Jim Healy relied. Our true power, according to Spinoza, comes from understanding one's place in nature. As natural beings, we derive our strength from nature. Unfortunately, we cannot maximize and enjoy this power as long as we fail to understand it properly. Most of us tend to think of power in the way that Jim Healy thought of it, strength over something or control over another person. In either case, we mistakenly believe that power originates with us.

In reality, we do not generate power; we receive it. This is clear if we simply observe the beating of our hearts or the pumping of our lungs. We depend on the force of nature, the life force, to sustain us. But this force is not limited to basic physiology. According to Spinoza, it is responsible for everything we do and feel, including our emotions.

Unfortunately, most of the time we misunderstand our emotions. When
we misunderstand emotions, when we misidentify their real causes, we
deceive ourselves into thinking that we are in control of our lives when,
in fact, our emotions are controlling us. Spinoza makes this point with
striking examples when he writes:

> A baby thinks that it feely seeks milk, an angry child that it freely seeks
> revenge, and a timid man that he freely seeks flight. Again the drunken
> man believes that it is from the free decision of the mind that he says what
> he later, when sober, wishes he had not said. . . . So experience tells us
> no less clearly than reason that it is on this account only that men believe
> themselves to be free, that they are conscious of their action and ignorant
> of the causes by which they are determined.[3]

Only by adequately understanding our emotions and what causes
them can we direct our lives and live in accordance with our own true
nature. This is how we become our true selves, and this is where our
real power lies.

This is a second paradox of power. We become most powerful not
by exerting our strength over others, but by opening ourselves to the
force of nature. To realize this strength, we have to let go of the idea
of ourselves as the center of concern so that we can attune ourselves to
the source of our real power, which comes from outside of us. In psychological terms, we have to de-center the ego to become grounded in
the larger self of nature.

For Jim Healy, we can see how much work this would entail. Having
been forced from his home and family at a young age by poverty, he felt
as if he had little control over his life. With each day that he worked,
each dollar he earned, and each meal he ate, his sense of control over
his life increased. When the responsibilities of fatherhood came along,
the urgency for control became greater. He did not, however, have the
time or the inclination to work at understanding how his childhood experience might be driving his adult behavior or his approach to parenting. As the person of authority in the house, he acted on emotions and
inclinations that were churning in the dark inside him. Hidden from the
light of reason, he had little understanding of his emotions. They controlled him while he thought he was controlling his son. All the while,
his son was building up his own reservoir of emotional turmoil, which
led him down a path of self-destruction. It was not until Sean came to

Jim with insurance papers to enter drug rehab that he was forced to abandon the idea that he could control his son's life.

All parents must negotiate a balance between setting rules for children and leaving them alone to develop in their own unique ways. In order to do this effectively, parents need to understand the role of power and authority. The most difficult work is to gain an adequate understanding of our own emotions so that they are not controlling us while we think we are controlling our kids. If we understand that our real power is realized by finding our place in nature, by being true to ourselves, which is possible only by understanding our emotional lives, we can avoid many of the painful and destructive battles that constitute so many relationships between parents and children. For parents, then, it is an important turning point when we use reason to understand our own emotions rather than blindly wielding power to control our children.

The relationship between Jim Healy and his son, Sean, is worth examining because Jim was not simply a brute. Like the rest of us, he did not master all of his emotions, and he misunderstood the nature of power and how to use it as a father. But he was also a man of principles. While the attempts to exert direct control over his son were doomed to fail, they were softened by his dedication to provide for his family and by his commitment to principles that led him to return a bag of free money. These lessons were transmitted to his son, also. It was because he had these qualities that Sean could turn to him when he finally admitted he needed drug rehab. And upon achieving sobriety, Sean discovered that these qualities had become a part of his character. While Jim might have squeezed his son too tightly in some ways, his principles indicated a healthy control over important aspects of his own life.

For us, one lesson to be learned here is that we do not want to be forced to examine our own emotional lives only when our children present us with papers to enter drug rehab. Jim Healy was a dedicated father, a princely neighbor, and a powerful worker. All of these great qualities could not spare him the pain of seeing his son follow a path of self-destruction. No matter what great qualities we may have, we must be vigilant in understanding ourselves, in particular our emotions, because without this understanding, we are not in control of our own lives. When we lack control of our own lives, we misunderstand and misuse the authority and power we have over the lives of our children.

2

ADVOCACY

The world is not always fair, and an important responsibility of parents is to stand up for their children when they are being treated unfairly. Sometimes children are treated unfairly by other children, and sometimes nature treats them unfairly with illnesses and other impediments to health and happy living. Under these circumstances, one of the primary responsibilities of parents is to advocate on behalf of their children.

On the other hand, the emotional bonds between parents and children make it difficult for parents to stand back and let their child handle the bumps and bruises of life. Some of these bumps and bruises are critically important for children to endure if they are going to develop the personal mettle necessary to function effectively in a tough adult world. Overly protective parents tend to overadvocate on their children's behalf and shield them from wounds that are an essential part of growing up.

In this chapter we meet parents who advocate in very different ways. Some advocate appropriately and some inappropriately, while others simply let their children cope with disappointment and hurt, recognizing that there are important life lessons to be learned from working through pain and that strength grows out of adversity.

NECESSARY ADVOCACY

One of the most fortuitous and fortunate meetings of my life occurred
when I was a student at University College Dublin (UCD). Early in the
school year I showed up at a meeting for the basketball team, but decided after the meeting that I had played enough basketball and didn't
want to commit to another season of practices and travel. I floundered
around Dublin for a few months after that meeting with Wittgenstein
as my private companion, until one day I noticed a posting on the bul-
letin board in the student center with my name on it asking me to call
about basketball. Not realizing the note had been there for a couple of
months, I reconsidered the pros and cons of joining the team. At the
minimum, I would get some exercise and some human contact, so I
decided to call. I vividly remember the first practice I attended, turning
to the person behind me on the layup line, gesturing to his shirt and
asking "You went to Dartmouth?" Pleased with the acknowledgment,
he smiled and nodded.

Luku Cullen was studying Irish literature at UCD and would eventually write an exquisite master's thesis on the work of John Banville.
Along the way he would sing spontaneous rap songs in Dublin pubs on
St. Patrick's Day, fight on the UCD boxing team, and clear men from
the lane in basketball games as we steamrolled to the University championship. I had never met anyone with a mind as sharp and versatile as
Luku Cullen's. Trips to games were filled with conversations about Co-
pernicus and Newton as he spun riveting explanations of what Banville
was doing in his novels. In passing, he would interrupt a monologue
to denounce a racist joke or comment by a teammate with a piercing,
acerbic wit that shamed those who didn't know better. Everyone knew
better in short order. As it turned out, Luku lived only a few miles from
me in New York. After returning from Dublin we would become close
lifetime friends.

In the months after returning to New York, we both struggled with
questions about the best career to pursue. Luku traveled a bit and ended
up at the University of Chicago, one of the country's premier Ph.D.
literature programs. He breezed through the program, distinguishing
himself in the eyes of his professors but internally unconvinced that the
academic life was for him. Having finished all of his coursework and

contemplating the prospect of a dissertation, he rented a moving truck one day, drove eighteen hours back home, pulling into his girlfriend's driveway in the middle of the night without stopping until the top of the truck crashed into the roof of the front porch. He had left Chicago behind and was faced, once again, with the question of what he would do with his life.

Luku has since become a lawyer, but, as you might guess, he is no ordinary lawyer. I don't learn that from him. He rarely discusses what he does. So it was to my surprise and pleasure that I found a striking dark envelope in my mailbox before Christmas with his firm as the return address. I opened the envelope to find beautifully produced brochures documenting four cases that Luku had worked on since he established the public service department of his law firm. In each of these cases, Luku fought for the rights of people who were being ignored and neglected by the systems in which they lived. These cases ranged from supporting foundations that are building medical schools in Africa to helping businesses rebuild after Hurricane Katrina.

Then there is the case in which Luku served as counsel and advocate for Jenna Flaubert, a young woman burdened with the challenges of being born premature at four and a half months, and having cerebral palsy and quadriplegia. Jenna has always required assistance to perform the basic physical tasks such as eating, dressing, and moving around, and she has difficulty speaking. Unfortunately, the school system couldn't see beyond her physical challenges. They simply assigned labels to her and dismissed her as unteachable. But in doing so, they were unable to see what Luku saw as "awesome potential." Thankfully for Jenna, her mother was a fierce and unrelenting advocate who also knew Jenna's potential and was determined to help her to realize it. She began fighting for Jenna when the New York City Board of Education dumped her into a class with every other local kid who had a disability. With so many different children facing very different challenges, it was impossible for any of them to get adequate attention. Jenna's mother knew she had to step in as an advocate for her daughter, but she also knew that fighting the Board of Education bureaucracy would be a monumental task.

Things took an unusual turn for the better after September 11, 2001, when Jenna and her mother were forced to flee their Battery City apartment. They moved in with Jenna's grandmother in Connecticut, where she entered a public school that did not label her and cast her off as unteachable. Instead the students and teachers worked with Jenna and she began to make the progress her mother knew was possible all along. Thankfully, just before September 11, Jenna and her mother had teamed up with Luku Cullen to challenge the Board of Education regarding their neglect of Jenna and her educational needs. Determined to help Jenna realize her potential, Luku fought and won monumental and crucial legal decisions on her behalf, which resulted in compensating the Flaubert family for the cost of educating her while living in Connecticut. As Luku put it, "The Board of Education saw the wheelchair, they saw her CP, they saw her quadriplegia, and they folded the book when they should have been . . . teaching Jenna how to read the book."

Along with Jenna's mother, Luku not only saw Jenna's potential; he also saw her as a unique and special person. He was demonstrating the hidden depths of the face-to-face relationship that twentieth-century French philosopher Emmanuel Levinas so powerfully describes in *Totality and Infinity*.[1] In the face of the other, according to Levinas, we encounter a trace of the infinite. It is not the infinite itself we see in the face; our limited minds cannot handle that. But we can find glimpses of the infinite if we look carefully enough at the surface and the details that present themselves in those we meet in the flesh. The depth of other people is not immediately revealed, either in how they look or in what they say. It is hidden, and most often we fail to take the time to look more closely. And yet, if we did, we would realize that there is much more than we are capable of knowing or understanding behind the face, or the surface, of every individual.

To know that there is always more to the people we meet than we initially see is an important starting point for changing the way we relate to others, especially our children. When we don't understand them or when we don't approve of what is being revealed on the surface, we know that something is brewing beneath the surface. This knowledge might give us the patience to look and listen carefully to a child in order to decipher the causes and motivations of his actions. Inasmuch as the face of the other is the trace of the infinite, it is, according to Levinas, the basis of an obligation we all have to care for the other. That is to say, the primary building block of human relationship is not one of free choice wherein I choose what to do and where to go; rather, it is one of obligation to care for the other's well being. This obligation is in place before any choices can be made.

Parents are better able to understand Levinas' insight than most because they feel an indelible sense of obligation to care for their children. If they do not care for their children as infants, the children die. If they do not attend to their children as they grow, the children can get irretrievably lost. For children do, in fact, break through our self-centered concerns and force us to put them ahead of ourselves. Most parents welcome the obligation to care for their children and, in meeting this challenge, they are in a position to see the hidden or infinite depth of their children for themselves.

Whether or not one agrees with Levinas in identifying the face as a primal and inescapable sight of ethical obligation, his insight into the hidden depths that resides behind the face should caution us never to be satisfied with what we see on the surface.

Among Luku Cullen's many outstanding qualities, this is, perhaps, his most distinctive. He has the courage to look into the face of each individual, knowing that there is a hidden world to be uncovered, and, with a rare power of intellect, tenacity of spirit, and gift of eloquence, he brings that infinite world to life for those fortunate enough to have him as counsel, father, or friend.

When I read about Luku's work with Jenna, I was not surprised that he took on such a case or that he won. What those who read the press clippings documenting the awards Luku has won as a public service lawyer do not know is that he was fighting a similar battle as a father on behalf of his own daughter. Their daughter was diagnosed with a rare neurological disorder that emerged after she had entered elementary school, and Luku and his wife were faced with the challenge of a lifetime that would have consumed many of us with less willpower. Not only did the Cullens develop an expertise on the condition afflicting their daughter while consulting with the world's most qualified experts on the condition, but they also found themselves in a battle to provide her with the best educational protocols. This was Luku's first exposure to the shallow hubris of some public education systems; like Socrates in ancient Greece, however, he became the gadfly that stung the lumbering horse to wake it up.[2] The combination of logical rigor, legal expertise, and, perhaps most importantly, his ability to see and articulate the world from the perspective of his afflicted daughter was unconquerable. Like the hands of a craftsman that combines strength and skill, sensitivity and purpose, Luku's sensitivity to his daughter combined with his intellectual sharpness and rigor made those who heard him understand what it was like to see the world the way his daughter sees it, why the school system failed her, and what they needed to do to rectify their failure.

Luku Cullen is a powerful advocate for vulnerable children being neglected by the systems and circumstances in which they find themselves. Not only is his advocacy an embodiment of the wisdom parents need when trying to decide when they should advocate for their children, but it is an incarnation of the courage to pursue it. In this case, his advocacy was driven by his knowledge of the hidden potential waiting to be dug out and nurtured from beneath the labels thrown at the children. To all of us charged with the task of caring for children, Luku Cullen reminds us to turn to the child for our direction and motivation and not to accept or rest content with the labels our "experts" are all too willing to cast upon them. This is hard work, especially when we are tired, our patience is worn thin, and we long for some peace, certainty, and direction. In these moments, we want somebody to tell us what to do, to provide a solution, to make life easier. But in our calmer moments, we might remind ourselves that each child, each person in fact, reveals only a small part of who and what they are. That is all that any of us can reveal. The real task is to help others, especially our children, find a way to show as much of their hidden depths as they can. And this is an inexhaustible task, as each child is a trace of the infinite. If we don't see it, it is not because it is absent: we are simply not looking hard enough.

In witnessing Luku interrupt a rap song he was spontaneously composing or a discourse on Newtonian physics in a Dublin pub in order to check a teammate's racist joke, or wonder at his decision to join the boxing team with no experience, and play basketball while composing a commentary on Banville, I knew he had the gifts to be someone special in this world. Through his work as an advocate for children—his own and others'—he has turned out to be even more special than I could have anticipated. He stands out as a reminder to parents to turn toward the child and to avoid resting content with categories and labels that suppress their hidden depth.

PARENTING BY SUBSTITUTION OR MISGUIDED ADVOCACY

With the gray February afternoon winding down, I gathered the books from my desk, threw my book bag over my wool overcoat, and headed to the dean's office to reserve a meeting room for the following weekend. The secretary took out her calendar and, before she could pencil in my request for a room, a student came running into the office visibly upset and panting, "Where's the dean? Where's the dean?" Another office worker directed her to the dean's door as I made my reservation and left the office. I walked into the corridor and watched a stream of students filing out of a classroom to my right, several of them visibly upset, a few of them crying. A former student of mine was standing next to the door they had just exited and asked me if I could help, gesturing for me to come to the room. As I got close to the door, I heard a string of profanities being shouted inside. Through the doorway, I saw Professor Ryan, who was retiring at the end of the semester after forty years of teaching, standing quietly behind his desk in the front of the room. The yelling was coming from just inside the door and I leaned in to ask the student to watch his language. As I did, he jumped out of his seat and yelling, "You!" began punching me in the face, smashing my glasses and cutting the corner of my left eye. Recognizing he was not going to stop on his own, I dropped my book bag from my shoulder and knocked him to the ground, holding him for a few seconds in the hope that he would calm down. When I let him up, he turned toward me, spit in my face, and began kicking me repeatedly while yelling that I was a fraud and a failure. The dean had arrived to witness the second part of his assault and when I asked her if I could defend myself, she wisely instructed me to go to her office.

As I tried to stop the bleeding from my eye, several administrators came into the room to discuss what should be done. Some were trying to minimize the incident to avoid bad publicity while others quickly considered the legal ramifications. The dean called the local police and when they failed to arrive after several hours, she had security drive Professor Ryan and me to the station to file a report.

The student who assaulted me had had a similar outburst in my class two years earlier. He didn't like the direction of a class conversation and began to curse at me and his fellow classmates, calling them "all a bunch of fucking idiots." More recently, he assaulted two students on campus, one a female whom he threatened to rape. After each of these incidents, his father, a lawyer, fought the disciplinary protocols of the college in defense of his son. The fact that he remained a student after these previous incidents indicates that his father was quite effective. Hence, it was not a complete surprise a couple of weeks after the assault to find a package in my mailbox with legal papers indicating that I was being sued for five million dollars for intentionally causing the twenty-two-year-old college senior psychological harm.

While his father may have effectively spared his son from suffering the disciplinary consequences of his actions, he was less effective as a father. In playing the role of advocate on behalf of his son, he was unable to hear what the boy really needed. His son, it seems, went through life with a swelling rage inside. His father couldn't help him because he didn't bother to look or listen to the underlying sources of his son's problems. He needed more from his father than advocacy; he needed his father's understanding and guidance, which could only be offered if the father took time to listen to his frustration and his pain. The son needed to be supported and disciplined by his father, not simply represented. By overplaying his role as his son's advocate, he overlooked the underlying causes of his son's emotional turmoil and interfered with his son's ability to grow into a well-adjusted adult. He pursued this approach to the bitter end by filing a lawsuit instead of working with school officials and counselors to find help for his son. His son ended up leaving the college just months before his graduation.

While this is a striking example of misplaced parental advocacy, it seems to be a growing trend. I was reminded of this trend recently when I stopped in to see a former high school basketball coach. I found him watching a wrestling match inside the high school gym where he is now the athletic director. His gray hair didn't surprise me, but he had put on a significant amount of weight. When I knew him, he was tall, lean, and strong. He had played college basketball and seemed to keep himself in top condition years later when he coached me. But that was more than twenty years ago. And while I didn't think about it when I was playing for him, his physical stature was part of what commanded so much respect from all of his players and students. But there were other reasons: he was a tough coach who knew the intricacies of the game and could teach them well. He demanded full commitment from his players and respected those who made it. But he was also a sensible man, I thought, someone a young person would do well to emulate in life. I was curious how I would find him now, so many years later.

I walked the length of the gym and sat next to him on a bench. The fact that he didn't recognize me at first reminded me that he wasn't the only one whose appearance had changed. With an authentic half-smile that made me feel welcome he said, "I thought you were some parent coming over to talk about his kid." "You get a lot of that these days, I guess." "Yes," but he did not elaborate for the moment. We talked on the surface about people we knew, our kids, and work, which led me to ask why he left Saint Mary's, where he was my coach. He told me the maddening story about a young principal that came on the scene a few years ago. He happened to be a classmate of mine who was ruining the school and teachers' lives with cronyism and capricious decisions and firings before he himself got ousted by the Board. In the meantime, Bert found himself a more stable position at Middle Prep, a highly respected suburban school run by Christian Brothers. As we talked, I mentioned that I was getting an itch to coach, probably from watching my girls play Catholic Youth Organization basketball. Never one to overreact, he gently encouraged me to consider coaching. I told him I would think about it, but I had reservations based on my observations of the way parents interfere with their children's coaches. He shared an incident he recently dealt with on that very issue.

Two years earlier, the freshman basketball team at his school won just two games. The following year four outstanding freshmen entered the school. The coaches, along with Bert, decided they would move these players to the junior varsity team, last year's unsuccessful freshman team. They thought these new players would improve faster by playing against older players and at the same time strengthen the team. All four freshmen started on the JV team, displacing four starters from the previous freshman team that won only two games. The team improved dramatically as it won most of their games. But this didn't please the parents. They wanted their kids to play more, as they had the previous season when they were losing. One mother was persistent in getting her husband to organize the parents to protest the coach's decision to play the freshmen more than their sons. The father agreed and used his skills as a litigator to convince the other parents that they had a case to make against the coach and the athletic director. With the other parents' support, he made an appointment for them to meet with the coach and the athletic director. He spent several hours preparing a "case" on behalf of his son and a few of his teammates before the meeting.

Bert's response to the parents was typically direct and honest. He understood their concerns, but made it clear that their children's private and short-term interests were not in line with the interests of the athletic program, the school, and, in the long run, their children. In order for a school to serve its function of educating students, he reminded them, there must be some common principles at the core of the institution. In this case, fairness, a derivative of truth and honesty, needed to be upheld against the private interests of a few disgruntled parents. Without these basic principles, members of the school community would lose respect for the institution and for those who run it. Without this respect, the prospect of a good education would be greatly diminished.

By making the parents aware that there were other points of view to consider and some basic standards by which the athletic program operates, Bert was providing them and, by extension, their children with essential life lessons. Not only did he introduce them to other perspectives they had not considered, but he also forced the parents to reflect on what they really wanted for their children. He urged them to think about the message they were sending their sons by advocating for more playing time, even though they were not as good as the new players.

In response to such an eye-opening conversation, each parent was left to ask himself or herself what would have been accomplished for each child if he or she were successful in convincing or intimidating a coach to play a child who didn't deserve to play. How would the child get along with his teammates, and how would the coach regard him? Would he reach his potential as a player, and would the team reach its potential? If not, would he ever learn what it takes for him or his team to be as good as they can be? Where would he learn how to adjust to different roles as a member of a team or a group? Would he learn the truth about his abilities as a player so that he could make informed decisions about how to spend his time in the off-season? Should he work on his game, hoping for a chance to play again on the varsity team, or should he turn his attention to some other activity that might serve him better in life? And, perhaps most importantly, would he begin to doubt himself and his ability to succeed in life because his parents doubted his ability to compete and to improve now?

Children are best served when they get honest answers to these questions and when they can answer them honestly for themselves. When parents advocate for their children on the wrong principles and for the wrong ends, they hinder the development and maturity of their children. Rather than move them along toward healthy adulthood, they are inserting obstacles that their children will eventually need to overcome if they are to realize their potential as human beings.

In this particular case, Bert had a follow-up story that made it easier to for the parents to accept the truth he had just shared with them about their sons. Bert's own sons are athletic stars, his oldest a professional baseball player. His second son is a college player at one of the best baseball programs in the country and as a freshman earned a starting spot at third base. About ten games into the season, he made an errant throw to first base, pulling the first baseman off the bag and allowing the runner to be safe. After the game he told his father, "I'm done." "What do you mean you're done? It was one throw that was a little wide. Why would you be done?" his father asked. "You'll see," his son replied with no more explanation. His son, full of promise as a starting freshman, was replaced by a senior the next game. The senior played well for the remainder of the season and his son didn't start the next forty games. Bert and his wife agonized for their son, although they couldn't dispute coach's decision. The senior was giving his coach no reason to sit him down. The freshman would have to wait until he was a sophomore for his chance.

The parents of the high school basketball players realized they were talking to a person who knew what they were going through because he had gone through it with his own son, who was a player of much higher ability than their sons. They also knew that Bert, who was a person of integrity, was presenting them with the opportunity to make an important turning point in their lives as parents. As much as we love our children, we bear a responsibility to develop the qualities they need to live a good life on their own and for themselves. We need to recognize that they have to work to succeed on their own merit, not because we arrange special favors for them. These parents were learning that it was time for them to step back as advocates for their children. Even though it was being done out of love, this advocacy was misguided and, ultimately, not helpful to their sons. Bert was doing them a great favor in forcing them to let their sons be themselves, to make it on their own merits and, hopefully, finding a belief in the resilience of their children that would help their children find themselves.

Upon hearing how he handled the parents who came to advocate for their sons, I was reminded of his integrity and reassured to know that he is still teaching timeless lessons about growing up, about responsibility, commitment, and honesty to those who cross his path. For parents, he represents a turning point at which they must begin to trust in their children, in their ability to learn from mistakes, and to earn what they get instead of overadvocating for empty rewards.

LETTING BE

The college where I teach is beginning the process of searching for a new president for the first time in twenty years. The steering committee that is initiating the search invited a group of faculty to a meeting to discuss the needs of the college and the desirable qualities of a new president, as well as the search process itself. Several concerns and ideas were raised, ranging from the need for a bigger endowment to the quality of students that were being admitted to our school. At one point a member of the steering committee asked the assembled faculty members what brought them to the college. As far as I could tell, the question was never answered directly, although several faculty members did take the opportunity to indirectly congratulate themselves on the fine work they were doing as teachers, and describe how much they love working at the college.

I wasn't surprised by the turn in conversation or by the fact that there was little concern for answering the question that was asked. I had heard these sentiments several times before. In fact, I was one of two speakers at a seminar on teaching at the college wherein the other speaker spent several minutes telling the group about how proud she is at the end of a semester when she sees how much knowledge she transports from her mind to their minds. She says to herself, "Look at what I did," as if the students were empty vessels that she simply filled with her knowledge. I suspect my colleagues are not different from faculties around the country. Professors tend to have high opinions of themselves and inflate the effectiveness and quality of what they do. In my experience, there are some faculty that work hard and are dedicated to teaching, while others treat their career as downtrodden civil servants who try to get as much as they can for doing as little as they can. And so, whether it is because they are defensive about what they do and don't do or because they just don't know any better, many teachers and institutions overestimate the quality of education they are providing students today.

As I drove home, the frustration of the meeting quickly faded and I began to cheerfully anticipate walking through the door of my house to hear the chattering voices of my three children coming at me all at once, with different tones, a different sense of urgency, and different concerns that reflected their different ages. Since I was later than usual, I was also prepared for the possibility that these three different voices might have worn thin my wife's patience. But I also looked forward to being able to relieve her from being the target of their limitless needs and energy. As I entered the house, there was a calmness that initially felt very comforting, but quickly raised suspicion that something was being hidden. My two daughters looked settled on the couch: their hair was drying from a shower as they wrapped themselves in their favorite blankets. I asked them how they were and both said fine, although my oldest daughter, Caitriona, looked to her younger sister, Anna, with a genuine sense of concern as she answered. When I looked more closely at Anna, it was clear that her beautiful soft, dark eyes that naturally carry the trace of a smile in them had just been cleansed by tears. "Are you okay, Anna?" I asked. "Yes," she responded softly. Before I could ask why she was sad, my wife summoned me to the kitchen.

Caitriona and Anna are students at the Hoff-Bartlesson Music School. Caitriona, who plays the violin, has been there for four years and Anna, who plays the piano, is in her second year. Periodically, the school hosts recitals at which students give public performances. Caitriona has played in several of these and Anna in just a couple. They had never played in the same recital, although they were scheduled to do just that in a couple of days. They had both received outstanding report cards from school a week before and my wife and I decided we would treat them after the recital with a hot chocolate and a dessert. We were all looking forward to it.

I was particularly interested in seeing Anna perform because I had been taking her to her lessons each week throughout the year and watching her progress. Until recently, I sat in the room during her lessons, but I had to stop for a couple of reasons. One reason is that I wanted to use that hour to do some of my own work. The more decisive reason that I stopped sitting in, however, was that I couldn't take the pressure. Usually Anna would arrive early, take off her coat, sit up on the piano bench, and begin to play a piece of music. Those notes were the most beautiful sounds I could ever imagine hearing. There was my eight-year-old, controlling the keys of a grand Steinway with rhythm and grace. I was happy and incredibly appreciative for what Ms. Crawford was doing with Anna.

Ms. Crawford is a serious teacher, pleasant but not chatty. She takes every minute of the lesson seriously and, while she is very warm and welcoming, she also is uncompromising in her expectations of what Anna should do. Anna's lesson is on Monday evenings from 6:45 to 7:30, and at the age of eight she sometimes tires toward the end: her concentration lags, she takes longer to answer basic questions, and makes more mistakes. As she fades, my anxiety builds, wishing her to get the next attempt right while at the same time wishing Ms. Crawford to end the lesson on time, something she rarely does since she is so committed to fitting as much as possible into each lesson.

One particular night, Anna's tiredness set in and she was having a difficult time perfecting the rhythm of "Bagpipe Dance" by Felix LeCouppey, a nineteenth-century French composer. To help Anna recover the proper beats, Ms. Crawford had Anna join her in tapping the beats of the tune on the face of the piano. Anna's light and delicate hands kept time with Ms. Crawford's strong and sure hands as they counted out loud and beat the rhythms of the piece into the piano. She then directed Anna to play it again. The contrast in sound between hands slapping wood and the notes that emanated from the open piano was rewarding, like candy for my ears. It was now 7:40, a full ten minutes past the time the lesson was scheduled to end. Anna was playing through the piece and made it to the last line without a blemish. I was listening and hoping, silently willing her to the end. She made it to the last note, which was intended to be held for eight beats, but lifted her finger too soon. Without hesitation, Ms. Crawford said, "Very good, but you didn't hold that last note long enough." She pointed to the beginning of the second to last line of the piece and said, "Start here."

It is hard to describe the unusual mixture of feelings I had at that moment. On the one hand, my anxiety built because I thought Anna was getting worn down, frustrated, and on the verge of getting upset. But along with my anxiety, I had a respect for Ms. Crawford that was so strong I was in a genuine experience of awe. These days there is hardly an organizational mission statement that doesn't boast a "commitment to excellence," even though few actually hold to it. In this room, however, I was witnessing an authentic commitment to excellence of which my daughter was the beneficiary. Anna herself hasn't yet fully internalized that lesson as well as she has internalized some of the pieces of music she has learned. But she will if she is to stay with Ms. Crawford because that lesson underlies every music lesson she gives Anna.

Ms. Crawford's commitment to uncompromising standards pervades the entire school at Hoff-Bartlesson. One of the ways they help students is by giving them opportunities to play with and in front of their peers at "informals." It is on these occasions that an instructor other than the student's primary teacher listens, teaches, and critiques the students on the pieces they play. These instructors also provide a written report to the student's primary teacher. The school tries to schedule students to do an informal shortly before their recitals in order to enhance their preparation. Anna had her regular lesson on Monday, an informal on Tuesday, and her recital with Caitriona on Thursday. On Monday, Ms. Crawford told me after the lesson that she played all of the notes correctly but her rhythm still wasn't perfect. She should work on it before Thursday, and if she still had trouble she should concentrate on playing the piece correctly for the recital even if the rhythm wasn't perfect.

I took Anna to her informal Tuesday evening. I sat in the car and read while she listened to her peers and played for them and the instructor. I was outside the room when Anna came out with cookies in her hand, a treat the school offers the students at each recital and informal. "Five cookies," I said, mixing surprise with a tinge of disapproval. "I got some for you. Here," she said, as she extended a hand full of Milanos. "How did it go?" I asked, with more interest than usual, knowing Ms. Crawford would also be interested to hear how she handled the rhythm of the piece. "It was fine," Anna said in her cheerful carefree way and characteristically started into the details of a story about what she and a friend did at school that day.

"What happened?" I asked my wife quietly as I followed her to the kitchen. "Ms. Crawford called from Hoff. Anna can't play in the recital." "Why not?" I asked. "She's not ready." "But she said everything was fine last night when she came out of the informal." "Apparently not. The instructor at the informal said she wasn't ready." I was surprised, because I heard Anna play the piece and, while I am not a musician, I can tell when a piece sounds good and when it doesn't. And while I can sometimes overappreciate the merits of my children's music, I did think her piece sounded as good as many of the other children that play in recitals. "Don't say anything," my wife pleaded. "She's upset. She cried as hard as I've ever seen her cry when I told her." I returned to the living room where the girls were watching television. Anna's eyes showed uncertainty, mainly, I think, because she was concerned about how I would react. I asked them what show they were watching. They were both happy to give me the details to keep the disappointing news out of the conversation. Anna was relieved when I stood up to leave the room. Our plans to honor their achievements after the recital would be put on hold.

We arrived at the recital and the director greeted us and asked where Anna was. We reminded her that she was told that she wasn't ready. "Oh yes," she recalled, "her rhythm was off on Monday. It sounded a little strange." Her wide, welcoming smile, combined with a sureness in her words, reminded me of what Emerson described as "good-humored inflexibility."[3] She continued, "Better to find it out there than here." We sat and listened to all of the students, including Caitriona.

The hour-long recitals at Hoff are one of my favorite entertainments. Some of the students are very young and just learning; some are hard working students who methodically perfect pieces of music at a steady pace through the years; and some are musical geniuses that can move one to tears when they put bow to string and generate sounds that pierce the shell of one's personality, prodding dormant feelings to life, as the violin of twelve-year-old Hannah Rhodes did to me this night. Caitriona played as well as she has ever played, demonstrating once again one of her most notable gifts: to be able to perform better than she practices. After listening to each of the students, my wife and I agreed that Anna's piece was as good as some of the students at a comparable stage in their education and that the decision to move her recital back seemed a bit cautious. And then my wife reminded me that Ms. Crawford called three times after delivering the news that Anna could not participate in the recital to make sure she was okay. And in each of those conversations, Ms. Crawford reiterated her thoughts on Anna. "If she wants to play music for herself and for her own amusement, that's fine. But Anna has the talent, the coordination, and the music inside of her to play at a very high level."

Without elaborating, it was clear that the standards to which Ms. Crawford holds her students are the standards that the students bring to her. And she is unwilling to compromise those standards. She is a teacher with the highest integrity, and she is a gift to Anna and to all the students who get the chance to study with her. During one conversation in which Ms. Crawford was checking on Anna, my wife thanked her for not moving Anna along before she was ready, for being honest about where she was, and for sticking to her standards for excellence. And Ms. Crawford replied in characteristic simplicity, "I appreciate that." I suspect that teachers of such unusual integrity are not often recognized for what is most important to them and most difficult to uphold: an uncompromising commitment to standards, to achieving the highest possible outcome that the student is capable of.

Ms. Crawford has reminded me that I should not be overly impressed by the accomplishments of my children just because they are mine and I love them. She also reminded me that there is no offense in speaking the truth, even when that truth is not what someone wants to hear. From her I was reminded that it is people who strive to do their best that I admire most. Those who do not compromise standards and do not pass pupils along because it is expedient are the ones parents should seek out, and when we find them, we should listen and learn from them.

They show us that our minds are best directed to the search for truth, which requires honesty on the part of the seeker. To be honest with someone is a sign of respect. Ms. Crawford respects herself, her profession, and the music and the composers she teaches; and she respects Anna. Whether or not Anna becomes an accomplished pianist is not as important as the life-long lessons she is getting by having a prolonged relationship with an accomplished teacher who shows Anna respect by demanding the best from her. Anna will forever know the difference between people who are honest and genuinely strive for excellence and those who merely talk about it. She will also know the difference between those who treat her with respect and those who do not, as a result of studying with Ms. Crawford.

I tell this story with a touch of envy as I think back to the meeting I was at when Anna got the call that scratched her from the recital and caused tears to erupt from a well of disappointment. If only the professors gathered around the large mahogany table were as focused, dedicated, and honest as Ms. Crawford. If only they respected the students and the parents that pay for them to be at a private college as much as Ms. Crawford respects Anna and, by extension, us. If only they shared her commitment to truth and honesty. If only people like Ms. Crawford and schools like Hoff-Bartlesson were the norm and not the exception. Instead, after more than an hour of conversation between a group of faculty and members of a presidential search committee, the issue of academic excellence was scarcely mentioned. It is impossible for me to imagine Ms. Crawford lapsing into a self-congratulatory speech about what she does for her students. She's not interested; she doesn't have the time. Her next student is waiting at the door, and she's already running past her lesson hour to make sure the last note of her student's piece is held for all eight beats as the composer intended.

Aristotle, perhaps the greatest of all philosophers, famously wrote that the right thing to do is found in the mean between excess and defect, between too much and too little. He also recognized that the mean would be different for each person and every situation. It is the person of virtue and practical wisdom that can identify and strike the mean in actions and thoughts, which is why cultivating a virtuous character is critical, according to Aristotle, if one is to live a good life. As parents, it is a constant challenge to find the proper balance between excess and defect when dealing with our children, their peers, their schools, teachers, coaches, doctors—and the list goes on. Nowhere is practical wisdom, the ability to choose the mean between excess and defect, more valuable than in the art of parenting and, in particular, in finding the proper balance between advocating for our children and letting them work through life's challenges on their own. The stories in this chapter show a range along a spectrum from ardent advocacy to holding one's tongue and simply letting things be. The wise parent is the one who knows when and how to advocate for children by keeping in mind long-term and short-term consequences when deciding when to stand in and when to stand down.

3

GUILT

Will Bookman's twelve-year-old daughter, Emily, was preparing for her seventh grade final exams. Will had promised Emily and his wife, Laurie, that he would help Emily study in the evenings when he got home from work. Emily and Will agreed to start Monday evening so that they would have a full week of preparation before the exams began. Monday came and Will arrived home tired, but ready to work. Before going to his room to change clothes, Will asked Emily if she had organized her study materials. Emily assured him that she had. "Great," Will said, "get everything set up and I'll be down in a minute." While Will was in his room changing, Emily unloaded mounds of paper haphazardly stuffed into folders from her backpack. She quickly tried to arrange them in some kind of order before her father returned, shuffling a few papers into this pile and a few more in that pile.

Feeling rejuvenated after changing clothes and washing up, Will rolled up his sleeves as he hopped down the stairs to join Emily for some serious work. Upon entering the room, he began, "Okay, let's get to . . ." Will stopped in midsentence when he saw the messy piles of paper scattered across the table. "I thought you said you had everything organized." "I do," Emily replied. "This doesn't look organized to me. It looks like two messy piles of paper. Do you have a study guide for the

exams?" "Yes," Emily responded. "Where is it?" asked Will. Emily began to fumble through the papers on the table. Unable to locate a study
guide, Will interrupted her search to ask, "What exam are you studying
for first?" "It doesn't matter which one I study for first. The exams are
a week away. I have time to study for whichever one I want," Emily re-
torted, growing impatient with her father. Emily's tone reminded Will
just how tired he was, and he found himself making a conscious effort
to maintain his composure. After a deep breath he asked, "Why don't
we make a study schedule for the week using the study guides your
teachers gave you?" "I don't need a schedule. I already know what I
have to do," Emily insisted. "Fine," said Will. "What is your first exam?"
"Social Studies." "Okay, what are some things you need to know for Social Studies?" Will asked. "I don't know. I didn't study it yet." "But you
told me you know what you need to study." After a momentary pause,
Will made a suggestion, "I'll tell you what, you take an hour to get your
papers organized and then, together, we will look at what you need to
know." He left the room and headed for his office, where he answered
some e-mails from work.

An hour later, he invited Emily into his office and asked her to show
him what she had done. She was still unable to give Will a basic study
plan for a single subject. Will had lost his patience at this point. He
began to yell and his loud voice filled the room. "Are you kidding me?
Do you think I have time to fool around with this stuff? That's it. You
go study on your own and fail your damn tests! But don't come crying
to me when you do. And if you fail, no, if you get below an eighty-five
on any one of your tests, you will do nothing—I mean nothing—fun this
summer. Now get up to your room and start working." Emily folded her
papers, stuffed them into her backpack, and left the room as quickly as
she could. She was crying. Will slammed the door behind her and returned to his work, but could not concentrate, adding to his frustration
and anger. "What is wrong with her?" he asked himself. "I can't believe
she refuses to study or even attempt to study. Maybe she needs to fail
and then she will wake up."

A few minutes later, Laurie entered his office. "What happened?" she
asked. Will explained that he asked Emily, twice, to simply organize her
papers to prepare for studying. He even gave her an hour to pull out her
study guides and tell him what she needed to know for her exams and

she couldn't do it. He had enough of Emily's laziness, he said, and told her to go do it on her own.

As Will was recounting the story to Laurie, his anger and frustration were being decisively overrun by guilt. He could feel his angry words losing their edge and their meaning almost as soon as they passed through his lips. He now felt bad for making his daughter feel bad, for adding to her stress, and for making it more difficult to study. As he spoke, he realized that he actually did the opposite of what he said he would do—help Emily. In his mind, he now saw Emily's tears instead of a messy pile of papers. His assessment of Emily as lazy transformed to seeing her as young and uncertain. As his anger subsided and guilt emerged, he knew he had made a mistake. He would have to do something to fix it. Before speaking to Emily, he spent a few moments trying to see the situation from Emily's perspective and asked himself what Emily might be thinking and feeling as she headed into her final exams.

Rather than try to guess Emily's thoughts and feelings, Will turned inward to remember his own experience as a twelve-year-old. He quickly remembered the nervousness he felt before a test, the insecurity of asking for help, his lack of organizational skills. He recalled that those challenges were compounded by the struggle to fit in with friends, to conceal his feelings when he was left out or ridiculed, and the self-loathing he felt after ridiculing someone else. He also recognized that Emily faced even more difficulties as a young girl, in a different time, with so many more diversions and ways of fitting in or being left out. And she surely felt more pressure in school than Will did at the same age. In fact, Will's parents rarely stood over him while he did homework or studied for exams. If he simply passed his courses, his parents left him alone, and here he was telling Emily that if she didn't get above an eight-five in every class, she would be punished. It didn't take long for Will to realize that it was counterproductive to yell at Emily. The guilt he was feeling, he realized, was entirely appropriate.

Or was it? To some, Will's guilt may seem unwarranted since it is clear that Emily's study habits need to change. As her father, Will not only has the right, but also the obligation to be upset. One could argue that only a father who did not care would not be upset with the way Emily approached her studies. If Will simply told Emily that everything was fine, to continue what she was doing, he would be neglecting his responsibilities as a father. As we saw with parental power and advocacy, children and parents must go through difficult turning points if they are to become mature adults. By inserting himself as the one who finds her work habits unacceptable, Will is challenging Emily and, in doing so, causing hurt feelings. But it is a challenge that will benefit her, if she rises to meet it. Will also feels bad about his response because he listens to his conscience, which tells him he'd rather not hurt Emily's feelings, but Emily also needs to feel bad about her study habits if she is to make improvements. If Emily was fine with her study habits and Will did not let her know how he felt about them, he would be setting her up for failure.

Guilt is an essential turning point in the endless process of growing up, for both parents and their children. The first step in facing up to guilt is learning when and how to feel it. A healthy conscience is the basis of appropriate guilt, and parents have a critical role to play in the formation of a child's conscience. In particular, the expectations and standards a parent holds out for a child play an enormous role in what the child learns to be acceptable and unacceptable. Will's disapproval of Emily's study habits contributes to the development of Emily's conscience and, hence, her personality by establishing expectations and standards for her to follow.

As Emily sorts through the crossfire of hurt feelings, she will come to see these standards and expectations as the building blocks of her own conscience and reference points that she will rely on to make decisions throughout her life. Some of these reference points will shift as she develops her own identity and works though her own situations, and some will remain close to where they started out. Either way, they will serve as the bedrock of Emily's self-identity. They will shape her range of possibilities, of what to pursue and what to avoid. And she will know the difference between these poles of behavior based on how she feels in the aftermath of her decisions and actions. Her conscience will tell her when to feel guilty and when not to.

So on the one hand Will has an obligation to check Emily's study habits, and on the other he feels guilty for doing so. Like all parents, from time to time Will is faced with what seems like an intractable dilemma. Sometimes it seems as if we are condemned to feel bad about simply doing our job and meeting our obligations. In this rather ordinary story of a father losing his patience with his middle school daughter, we see just how difficult it is for parents with a conscience to find traction, to feel as if they are moving in the right direction.

The conflict between Will and Emily demonstrates that there are layers of ambiguity embedded in incidents that seem simple on the surface. This ambiguity makes it difficult for parents to know when we are acting appropriately and when they are not. The dissatisfaction and anger we might show in response to a child's actions are often followed by guilt when our child's feelings are hurt. These conflicting emotions can render us uncertain and incapable of providing decisive guidance to our children. In order to get beyond this debilitating ambiguity, and to use guilt as a turning point toward an authentic and mature adulthood, not only do we need to understand the different layers of guilt, but we also need the courage to face up to it. It might come as a surprise, which initially sounds downright depressing, to learn that guilt is something we never outgrow or completely leave behind. But even more surprising may be the claim that we don't *want* to leave it behind. Guilt is the turning point we must go through in order to live authentic lives, and authenticity is the central quality of an adult who has grown up.

REAL GUILT

In the language of Irvin Yalom, Will Bookman was feeling *real guilt*, which is the type of guilt we feel after a specific incident in which our actions, words, or thoughts leave us feeling at odds with ourselves and who we believe we should be.[1] Will wanted to be a good father by helping Emily with her studies, but he fell short of that goal when he yelled at her before understanding what might be holding Emily back from studying well. If he had sought this understanding before losing his patience, he would have been closer to his goal of helping Emily. Instead, his outburst made it necessary for him to backtrack from the task at hand—studying for her exams—to first repair their wounded relationship. Only after repairing the relationship would they be able to focus on studying.

Real guilt is a burden that we seek to get out from under as soon as possible because it has a negative impact on everything we do. When we are in the throes of real guilt, we carry with us a sense of disapproval. When we are guilty, we have no option but to acknowledge that another's disapproval of us is warranted. Feeling guilty, however, does not require another to disapprove of us. It is our disapproval of ourselves that burdens us the most. Real guilt leaves us feeling less worthy and less capable of being happy. Until we do something to turn this guilt around, it weighs on us, making everything we do more difficult. The unpleasantness of this weight makes it very tempting to hide from guilt rather than facing and fixing it.

Because of the intensely intimate relationships between parents and children, there are more opportunities for hurt feelings to occur each day than we can count. If we were to carry the heavy burden of guilt around with us after every conflict, we would likely be heading for the psychiatrist's office searching for a pill to keep us from despair. Most parents avoid this fate by becoming immune to the after-effects of minor conflicts in the home. This immunity is necessary to survive the intensity of our relationships with children with some degree of sanity.

On the other hand, guilt, although unpleasant, is not something to be ignored entirely, all the time. Because it is appropriate and even necessary to let go of many conflicts without taking them to heart, it is very tempting for parents to push aside or look past the negative feelings associated with guilt. Most of us have developed very effective methods of pushing guilt away so that we can get on with our day without feeling bad about ourselves. Just like the excuses we create to avoid physical exercise, even though we know it is essential for good health, we find rationalizations that suppress the feeling of guilt, even when it would be better if we didn't. We are all guilty of too often avoiding guilt. To counter this tendency, we first need to be aware of the tricks we use to do so.

THREE WAYS TO AVOID GUILT

I. Blame Somebody Else

The most common way of pushing away our guilt is to blame others. If we can convince ourselves that what we did was justified in some way, we might fool ourselves into thinking that we do not need to feel guilty. We do this by claiming that we know better than the other person does or by convincing ourselves that we are superior in some way. In other words, if I tell myself that I know better than the other person, whom I have offended or hurt, I might also convince myself that it is his or her lack of insight, awareness, or knowledge that caused dismay and not my actions. If the other was smarter or more insightful, this line of thinking goes, she or he wouldn't be offended. If I can convince myself that it is the other person's fault that he or she feels bad, I do not have to feel guilty.

2. No Choice

Another familiar way to suppress our guilt is to convince ourselves that whatever we did had to be done. The circumstances in which I found myself made my actions necessary; I had no choice. If there is no choice involved, I am not responsible for what I did. If I am not responsible for what I did, then I cannot be accountable for the way the other feels. Put another way, if the other person is offended by my words or deeds, he simply doesn't understand that I had no choice in the matter. My actions were inevitable. Once he understands this, he will no longer be offended. In the meantime, there is no need for me to feel guilty.

3. Superior by Comparison

Closely associated with the "no choice" or "it was inevitable" escape route is the "compared to him" escape route. This is the familiar way out that many parents take by comparing their parenting style or achievements with other parents. It also takes the form of imagining what other parents would do in a similar situation. The comparison method keeps guilt feelings at bay by telling oneself that no matter what mistake he might make with his children, he is still a better parent than the guy who drinks too much, or doesn't work, or is always mean to his wife and children.

Will could have taken any one of these familiar escape routes from guilt. As a father and a lawyer who has made it through school and successfully organizes himself at work each day, he certainly knows how to study better than his daughter does. He could easily use this knowledge to justify his response to Emily by telling himself that his daughter should listen to him if she wants to do well in school. If she chooses not to, she should then face the consequences. And as her father, he has an obligation to impose those consequences now so that she will learn and avoid more severe consequences later. In other words, he could view the interaction with his daughter in terms of black and white, right and wrong. He knows and she doesn't; therefore, he is right and need not feel guilty.

Will could also have taken the second escape route. He could try to avoid feeling guilty by blaming the circumstances. Being tired from a long day at work, his patience was thin. When Emily did not show the motivation and organization that he expected, it was inevitable that he would lose his temper. After all, he was doing her a favor on his free time. Emily needs to know that at some point, if she does not take responsibility for her work and continues to defy Will's expectations, she will have to deal with his expression of dissatisfaction. By convincing himself that such a response was inevitable, Will could absolve himself of responsibility for his actions and, theoretically, from his guilt.

The "superiority by comparison" method is, perhaps, the easiest and most common escape route parents use to avoid or hide from guilt. Will could call to mind his brother-in-law, for example, who pays no attention to his children's schoolwork. He simply arrives home from work, eats dinner, and turns on the television while the kids start and stop their homework several times each evening. Some of it gets done, some of it doesn't. Will's brother-in-law doesn't seem to care either way. He could also compare himself to his coworker who goes golfing almost every Saturday and Sunday, leaving all weekend responsibilities to his wife. Will could tell himself that he is at least making an attempt to help his daughter and showing a genuine interest in her studies. Even when he screws up, he is surely doing a better job than these disinterested dads. By convincing himself of his superiority over other fathers, Will could lessen or eliminate the guilt he feels as a result of the way he responded to Emily.

TREATING GUILT LIKE AN ITCH

If only it were so easy. Trying to cover over our guilt with these tactics is like scratching a mosquito bite. We might gain some temporary relief, but the itch returns, usually with greater discomfort. If we continue the cycle of scratching and gaining temporary relief, only to have the itch return, we end up with greater discomfort than we started with. Guilt is similar. Just as scratching a mosquito bite could work only if there were no skin beneath the bite, so that scratching would be the same as wiping it away, covering over guilt could work only if we didn't have a conscience. No matter how much Will Bookman might have tried to justify his response, whether by claiming superior knowledge, a lack of control due to circumstances, or comparing himself with others, his conscience would have been in the background, waiting for those voices to go silent. Once these voices fall silent, the voice of conscience would take the floor and it would not let Will off the hook until he took responsibility for the way he responded to his daughter.

In this case, Will's guilt might seem a little like a spilt soda. It was a relatively minor incident, but the lingering effect is like the sticky spot on the floor that we missed in the clean-up and now can't seem to avoid. We don't see the sticky remnants of the spill, but we feel it. While most parents can easily understand Will's frustration with Emily, and we have all responded to our children in ways equally severe or worse, we also know that incidents like this can weigh on us. The guilt we feel can ruin our day, or worse. As much as we would like to be able to leave guilt behind, it is not easy to do so. If we don't address it carefully, minor incidents can grow into major ones, like carrying the spilt soda to the new rug on the soles of our shoes. This is why it is critically important for parents to face their guilt and use it as a turning point, rather than avoiding it, if they want to continue to grow up.

CONSCIENCE AND INTRACTABLE DILEMMAS

This simple story of the interaction between Will and Emily demonstrates the ways we can experience and deal with real guilt in everyday family life. While most parents can identify with Will and how he responded, few would be overly concerned about such an incident. They happen all the time. Will managed to minimize this incident rather quickly by recognizing that he needed an alternative approach with his daughter. We all know, however, that it is not uncommon for minor incidents to lead to much deeper dilemmas and a more stubborn, entrenched experience of guilt.

This recently happened to Will's coworker, Steve Shannon, when a simple birthday request led to intense questioning about the direction of his life and the life of his family. The questioning was triggered when he felt compelled to set limits to his teenage daughter's birthday celebration. Ashley asked if she could go to a Broadway show for her sixteenth birthday. Steve and his wife, Janet, agreed. As the birthday came closer, however, Ashley typically began to request more for her birthday, including a dinner out with ten or twelve of her friends. This request aggravated Steve, not only because his daughter was being greedy, but also because he repeatedly heard Ashley complaining about several of the girls she wanted to invite. He happened to agree with the typical complaints of these girls as spoiled and cliquish. He had taken some of them out with his daughter before and found them shockingly unappreciative and disrespectful. In fact, after the last birthday dinner, he vowed to never do it again and he couldn't understand why Ashley would want to invite them to her party.

The decision to deny the added request for a large dinner party seemed simple enough except for the fact that Steve was sensitive to his daughter's struggle to find friends and fit in. He could see that she wanted to have birthday parties similar to her friends, even if it meant inviting girls she did not like and at a cost Steve and Janet could not afford. While Steve did not regret not being able to afford a dinner party, it did lead him to consider other material goods that he could not provide his family. He certainly could not afford the type of luxuries that the families of his daughter's classmates could. In addition to lavish birthday celebrations, many of these families took three vacations a year. Steve imagined how Ashley felt the first day back at school when they sat around talking about trips to Aspen or Bermuda.

Rather than simply condemn Ashley as spoiled or brush off the consumerism of his neighbors, Steve saw the birthday as an opportunity to teach Ashley an important life lesson about the value of friendships and the emptiness of short-term material rewards. While Steve and Janet did not have the material resources of many families in their community, they were proud of the things they value most and the choices they made to uphold those values. Janet decided to sacrifice her career and her handsome salary to stay home with her children. Steve could have pursued a career in finance, but it didn't interest him. In choosing to become a therapist, he chose a career that benefited others and excited him. He also wanted to work reasonable hours so that he could be present to participate in family life. In making these choices, they were aware that the pleasure and joy of life would have to come from something other than material rewards. As most parents know, this is not an easy message to get across to teenagers. Nonetheless, thinking it through with Janet gave Steve confidence that he made the right decision in denying Ashley the extra birthday celebrations.

And yet, despite this confidence, Steve found a nagging sense of guilt lingering in his gut. It was easy to deny Ashley an excessive birthday party, but what was he going to do about college tuition? He saw education as the key to a good life, financially and otherwise. Fearing he would not be able to afford the exorbitant price of a college education, he was overcome with dread when he considered that Ashley would be going to college in just two years. Because education was so important to him, the prospect of not affording it for his daughter led to a much deeper sense of self-doubt than simply denying a birthday party. When he considered his neighbors' ability to pay for their children's education out-of-pocket, he found himself reexamining his decision to pursue a meaningful career over one that was more financially rewarding. Maybe those who sacrificed their own interests entirely for the sake of a financially rewarding career were right and he was wrong. Maybe they were, after all, better fathers than he was.

A simple request from his daughter for a birthday party had plunged Steve into a deep sense of *existential guilt*, the type of guilt that never leaves, but is merely suppressed from time to time. Steve would come to know that this deep sense of guilt is an indelible part of the human condition and an essential turning point along the way to becoming an authentic adult and parent. How we deal with existential guilt plays a large role in the type of people we become.

INDELIBLE GUILT

If guilt is indelible, what are parents to do about it? Are we to simply accept that we are doomed to unhappiness? Or is there a way to deal with guilt that can make it work for us rather than against us? Since it is unpleasant, the natural human instinct is to avoid or eliminate guilt, and we have seen the methods we employ to do so. But the initial instinct to avoid or minimize guilt is not always in our best interest. Guilt is not simply one emotion among others that we experience in response to a mistake we made. It is as fundamental to who we are as the freedom we have to make choices. In fact, it is because we have freedom to make choices that we also have an indelible sense of guilt.

The freedom to make a choice makes us responsible for what we choose to pursue, and what we choose to leave behind. Once we choose one path, we forgo another. It is the sense of loss or emptiness resulting from leaving behind the paths we don't choose that contributes to our inescapable sense of guilt. This is the predicament of our human condition, which is both free and finite. We can't choose everything. But the freedom to choose among a limited number of possibilities, within a limited amount of time, is a predicament that presents us with the opportunity to be authentic. To turn toward authenticity, however, we need to hear the voice of conscience and embrace our guilt.

Unlike real guilt that arises in response to specific situations and actions, existential guilt resides at the base of our being, at the place where we choose to live an authentic or an inauthentic life.[2] This level of choice is deeper and more primary than ordinary choices we make in everyday life such as where to work, what to say to a child, or whom to befriend. The choice to be authentic or inauthentic requires a deep sense of silence so that the voice of conscience can emerge from beneath the noise of everyday life. Unfortunately, this is more difficult than it sounds. Many of us spend a good portion of our time seeking diversions from this quiet voice. This is one explanation of the obsession we have with television, computers, and all the other media that we allow to take hold of our attention and drown out the voice of conscience.

Why are we so afraid of this voice? It is not simply that we want to avoid the bad feeling that accompanies real guilt. It is the fear of accepting the awesome responsibility we have for our own lives. The voice of conscience reveals that we are responsible for choosing our lives at every moment of every day. The authentic person welcomes this responsibility and accepts the consequences of his choices. He doesn't blame others or his circumstances for his state of happiness or unhappiness.

He knows that the way he responds to any situation is his choice. He is also fully aware of what he is leaving behind when he makes a choice. The authentic father knows that his weariness did not make him yell at his daughter. Will Bookman's weariness and his daughter's behavior are the circumstances that presented him with a choice. That choice is authentic if he takes responsibility for it and the consequences that follow from it.

With the goal of authenticity in view, embracing existential guilt is not as morbid as it might initially sound. To embrace this guilt is not to walk around with our shoulders sagging, feeling badly about who we are. Nor is it to take on a neurotic guilt that imagines we are wrong and guilty when we are not. On the contrary, existential guilt instills a sense of urgency about life. It makes us aware of the importance of every moment and of every choice we make. This urgency is a trait of an authentic life. It is the lack of urgency, typified by a mindless stint in front of the computer or television that characterizes the inauthentic life.

The turn we make toward authenticity begins with the desire to have a conscience. At the level of real guilt, we feel bad because we are out of stride with what we believe we should be doing and because we must agree that any disapproval levied on or toward us is warranted. The individual who turns toward authenticity faces up to the bad feeling, takes responsibility for it, and works to reverse or eliminate what caused it. For Will, it was finding an alternative approach to studying with his daughter.

Existential guilt beckons us away from the noise and distractions of everyday life to hear the call of conscience. In silence, this call allows us to hear and see the choices that are most often hidden from us by the diversions of everyday life. The latest sitcom or video game numbs the urgency that comes with taking responsibility for choosing my life. For parents, this urgency is felt most deeply because they must not only choose a path for their own individual lives, but also choose the shape and direction of the lives of their children. As Steve Shannon discovered, it is an awesome burden to negotiate the choice of being true to oneself and doing what is necessary to provide for children. But it is the urgency of choosing that determines the level of authenticity in life. And, ultimately, it is this authenticity that will be among the most enduring lessons we pass on to our children.

Understanding the different levels of guilt and how they can serve as a turning point to achieve authenticity is critically important for parents who are faced with the responsibility of making important choices for themselves and their families. These choices are best made with a clear understanding of what we value most and an urgency to see those goods realized in our choices and actions. Choosing is often difficult because we must sometimes decide between goods that we value highly. For instance, Steve had to ask himself if he should stick with his career, which gave him great satisfaction while providing a service to others, or if he should pursue a path to greater financial gain so that he could afford college for his daughter. This is a difficult choice and nobody can give an answer that will work for everyone. But the authentic person makes the choice with the highest awareness and the greatest sense of urgency he can achieve. In doing so, he can easily take responsibility for the outcome of his choice.

Our response to guilt is a good indication of what we are most concerned about and value most. If we simply try to avoid the unpleasant feel of guilt, we are likely to seek a short-term fix to change those feelings. This is what leads parents to mindlessly buy more and more things for children, making them accustomed to short-term satisfaction found though material gratification. If, on the other hand, we are most concerned with raising children who will adopt values and standards to serve them well as adults, we will resist the temptation of short-term fixes and demonstrate the superiority of an authentic life. Those who courageously engage both real and existential guilt by listening to the call of conscience can take full responsibility for the choices they make in life. Rather than turn away from guilt, these mature adults and parents use guilt to turn toward authenticity.

4

COMMUNITY

"That's my favorite picture. Look James, there's you and me." Harry's eyes were wide with recognition as he pointed at the photo on the refrigerator door. "We're all wearing our Mets shirts," he continued. I turned from the counter to look down at the picture of five boys standing side-by-side in identical black tee-shirts with *Mets* inscribed across the front. To most people, it is an unexceptional photo of childhood friends. But it's not that simple. You see, my seven-year-old son, James, is one of the boys in that photo proudly displaying his support of his favorite team. And his favorite team is not my favorite team.

I grew up in the Bronx, and the team of my neighborhood and my family was the Yankees. I always took it for granted that a boy would accept his father's team as his own once he became interested in a sport. Passing on our allegiance to a hometown team, I thought, should be as natural as playing catch in the front yard. James and I play catch, although we root for different teams.

When James first started showing signs of waywardness, I didn't think much of it. I figured he was going through a phase and would come back to Yankee-land in good time. To make sure he didn't stray too far, I made certain that the first game he would see was a Yankee game. What seven-year-old could resist a trip to Yankee Stadium with seats just a few rows behind the Yankee dugout? I was sure this would convert him.

I remember the day well. As we got ready for the game, I was pleasantly surprised when he slid into his Derek Jeter jersey and Yankee cap without any objection. He saw the sense of blending in, I guess, but I thought his acquiescence was a sure sign that he was already switching affiliations. My plan was working.

We got to the stadium early to watch batting practice. Standing beside the Yankee dugout, Jeter, A-Rod, Posada, and most of the Yankees went through their pregame routine just a few yards in front of us. At first, James was excited but then disappointed because he wanted to go onto the field when he saw other fans chatting with Joe Torre. With the start of the game and a drink of lemonade, however, his disappointment faded quickly. We endured the hot day, cheering for the Yankees when we could, even though on this day there was little to cheer about: the Yankees lost. When the game ended, we lingered at our seats and gazed out at the hallowed field while the crowd filed out. I pointed to Monument Park behind the outfield fence, as I tried to convey to him some of the Yankee mystique rooted in heroes of the past: Babe Ruth, Joe DiMaggio, Mickey Mantle, Thurman Munson. James was attentive and as we turned to leave, I was confident my job was done. He would be a Yankee fan from this moment forward.

James said little as we made our way to the exit. When we got outside I told him to have one last look at the stadium and the list of their championship years painted on the façade. James paused and looked up. Without commenting, he turned away and we began to walk toward the car. A few strides in, looking straight ahead from beneath the arched peak of his Yankee cap, he finally spoke: "Dad, can we go to Shea?"

In response to our different baseball affiliations, I playfully think that Harry's favorite picture is not my favorite picture. My son proudly wears his Mets gear in the summer months while I occasionally don a Yankee cap. We joke about having different teams, and the photo is a reminder of this difference. But the photo represents something more important than our attraction for sports teams. James's affinity for the Mets is an early indication of the increasingly important role that communities outside the family play in the formation of a child's character. At an early age, their network of communities grows and our influence as parents is transformed, becoming less direct, less obvious, and, inevitably, simply less. His affection for the Mets stems from the influence of his friends and their tastes. It is more fun, or at least easier, for him to like the team that they like. As the only one in the photo without a brother, it makes even more sense that he wants to fit in with his friends on the block.

While choosing to root for a different sports team than one's father is an innocent example of how community influences the development of a child and the dynamics of a family, it is also emblematic of a much larger reality that parents are forced to negotiate, not only with and for their children, but for themselves too. Who we are, what we do, where we go, what we say, and even what we think are all shaped by the communities in which we live. Contrary to commonly held beliefs about human nature, there is no self, no individual, no private "I" that exists in complete separation from community.

This reality creates the perennial, multidimensional tension at the heart of every individual and every family. A child searches for an identity by relating to members of his family and those beyond his family. Parents create a family environment based on goods they value, although such goods are often at odds with the goods that are considered values outside the family. Parents must also negotiate the tension between their own development as adults while sacrificing their interests for the common good of the family. The way we handle this tension is crucial because it can serve as the model that our children are likely to emulate as they become progressively more independent and responsible for negotiating the tension for themselves. Moreover, the way we handle this tension is based in large part on how we understand the role of community in our lives as both individuals and as families. It is a real challenge for parents to resist the pull of social values that are at odds with their own values, especially when our children chip away at our resolve, as they press with incessant requests and strategies to wear us down. How we meet this challenge is, for parents, children, and families, a central turning point that takes us from the myth of individualism, parental control, and self-interest to the communal self and the common good.

CONTROLLING COMMUNITIES IN THE EARLY YEARS

In the first months and years of parenthood, before children begin to establish their own networks of friends, parents have the ability to choose the communities they will interact with as a family. This was the case for Jen and Jim Hartly, who were conscientious young parents in preparing and caring for their newborn. They were married at the age of twenty-seven. During the first couple of years of marriage, Jim completed his graduate studies in music while Jen managed the accounting department of a Manhattan public relations firm. Five years into marriage, Jen became pregnant for the first time. They planned well for their new arrival. Jen ate all the right foods and exercised regularly. They purchased a single-family home with a large, private backyard where they grew vegetables and flowers. Jen's preparation during her pregnancy paid off at the birth, as she delivered her baby girl naturally less than two hours after entering the hospital, and recovered quickly.

They approached the first months and years of parenting as they had approached most things in their lives, with ample preparation and commitment. After the early months of breastfeeding, they served only the best quality foods as they meticulously followed Jen's color-coded daily nutritional plan along with the appropriate supplements. Colic set in after a couple of months but was quickly rectified in consultation with their pediatrician, who was an expert on child nutrition. Aside from the standard lack of sleep, they were handling their first experience of parenting well.

The first significant disruption came when Jen had to return to work. Having spent six weeks with her newborn, the thought of leaving her for the entire workday was heartbreaking. She countered her sadness, which was often magnified by her tiredness, by planning and organizing the following day for her daughter each night before going to bed. In addition to writing detailed notes for Jim and other family members who cared for Suzie, Jen's routine included pumping the next day's supply of breast milk for her baby, a process that gave her little pleasure but that she endured, in part, because of the health benefits to her child and, less consciously, because of the attachment it sustained between her baby and her. Through her milk she maintained control over her baby's diet and, by extension, their relationship. She also took comfort in knowing that Suzie was with family while she was at work. When she wasn't with Jim, she was with members of their extended family. This arrangement seemed to work well, though years later Jim still holds a vivid image of his daughter banging on her grandmother's front door crying for him not to leave her as he walked to his car to drive to work.

Two years after Suzie was born, it seemed as if fate was on their side when Jen became pregnant with Kate, their second daughter. Two months into her pregnancy, news emerged that a large national firm would buy out Jen's company. The executives at her company were working on severance packages for the employees. The timing worked out for Jen so that she would get her maternity leave in addition to full severance pay, which was substantial. In addition to his teaching salary, Jim had earned significant income by giving private music lessons. It seemed that they were on sound financial footing when Kate was born, and this enabled Jen to become a full-time mother and pursue the priorities they had set for their children.

At the top of their list of priorities was the health of their children. Jim researched different approaches to health and medicine inasmuch as he was determined to protect his children from the perils and pitfalls of the mainstream American diet as well as some of the questionable practices of modern medicine. He and Jen found Dr. Nest, a pediatrician whose approach to medicine would support their priorities. Visits with Dr. Nest could last as long as three hours as the good doctor probed the circumstances of the child's world to learn as much as possible about the variables affecting her health. He wrote pages of notes during each visit and handed them to the parents at the end. Over time, these pages of information about foods, supplements, tonics, and books became a veritable library of pediatric health information. Jim and Jen had a deep trust in Dr. Nest and because of him became more knowledgeable and confident in caring for the children. For them, Dr. Nest was an excellent investment and became a central figure in their community, which was slowly expanding around their interests and concerns of caring for their children.

Another priority for Jim and Jen as parents was their children's education. From the very beginning, their primary concern was that their children develop their natural curiosity into a love for learning. Jen's research into preschools paid off when she found the Early Childhood Center (ECC) at a local college. The faculty at the ECC was made up of highly professional and experienced teachers. They all had a high level of emotional maturity combined with keen interpretive insight into the development of children, and also had assistant teachers who were graduate students engaged in studying education and child development at the college. The combination of youthful graduate students with experienced master teachers made for a fruitful educational dynamic. The environment they created compelled students to assume responsibility for their own learning and make a distinctive contribution to the class, whether through individual or group projects. The students learned by doing and decided what they would do as a group through discussions that the teacher guided. The activities that made up their day were geared toward helping students find and develop their own voice because the starting assumption of all faculty members was that each student voice had something important and creative to say. From the earliest days at the ECC, the children flourished.

Although there was no direct cause-and-effect correlation, it seemed that the better the children became at social interaction, the closer the parents of the children became. The community bonds that were forming in the classrooms were mirrored in the community of parents outside the classroom. Jim and Jen found their own lives enriched as a result of the friends they met through the school. Perhaps it is a coincidence that so many solid, insightful, and courteous people come together around a common interest, the education of their children, or perhaps it is the school environment that attracts such people, so that new parents discover the similar benefits in that community year after year. Over the course of the six years that Jim and Jen were associated with the school, they became friends with playwrights and bankers, musicians and teachers, bar owners and full-time mothers. What was most endearing about so many of these parents was their nonjudgmental openness and concern for others, qualities that came to the fore when one parent hit upon bad times.

This mother came to the United States with her husband to support his career. Three young children later, he decided to have an affair and left his wife without money and without citizenship. Parents at the ECC got together, quietly and without any fanfare, and worked to get her back on her feet. One parent bought the three children new clothes, tore off the tags so that they would look second hand, and delivered them to her home anonymously.

As Suzie's time at the ECC approached the end, Jim and Jen noticed that almost all of the parents were concerned with where their sons and daughters would go to school next. They recognized the difficulty of finding a school that replicated what they had experienced at the ECC. In light of the great control they had exerted over their choice of communities until this time in their children's lives, however, they weren't overly concerned. They assumed they could continue along the same path, find the right school, support their children as they had been doing, meet the teachers and parents associated with good schools, and enjoy the fruits of their choices as their children grew.

They identified a couple of schools that shared the ECC's educational philosophy. Their daughter tested very well and was accepted into these schools, but they quickly met an intractable roadblock as they moved forward: the tuition at these schools was more than $30,000 for kindergarten. They couldn't afford the tuition, especially for more than one child. They applied for financial aid, but were denied. For the first time since Jen had returned to work and left her first-born at home, they found community influences at odds with their goals. The private schools were unaffordable while the public schools in their town were unacceptable. After several weeks of resisting the facts, they decided they would have to move into a town with a "strong" public school. This set off more than a year of frustrating searches as the prices of houses climbed astronomically. They looked within a reasonable radius of work and family, while fully aware that whatever they found would constitute a compromise for their children's education. For the second time as parents, they faced a significant challenge to their ability to control the effect of community on their lives.

They finally found a small house that Jim, by building an addition, made livable, even though it was still one of the smallest in the neighborhood. As Jim and Jen settled in, they found their neighbors courteous and friendly. With very little traffic and several families with children close in age, their street provides the children an unusual amount of freedom. If one had an aerial view of the street at the end of a school day, it would look as if it came from a different era, as children swarm to the middle of the street to play basketball or baseball and look forward to the vintage 1965 Good Humor ice cream truck, which arrives every day at four o'clock, just in time to spoil their appetites for dinner. They roam in and out of each other's houses, the parents watchful and usually welcoming.

The idyllic façade of their local street community, however, is fissured with the inevitable tensions of living among families that one does not choose. In moving to a new community, we hope for the best with neighbors and settle for civility along with respect for property and privacy. But even when we are lucky enough to find these qualities in our neighbors, when it comes to children, it is inevitable that they will influence each other in ways that are at odds with things that are most important to us as parents. One parent believes that video games are detrimental to the healthy development of children and does not allow them into the home, while the neighbors see nothing wrong with them and keep the collection updated. The children gravitate toward the house with the video games. If a parent sticks to the video game prohibition, she finds her son isolated from the group. But differences in values can run much deeper. One family measures its success by its ability to show wealth, another by its academic achievements, still another by its moral outreach. These values and the families that adhere to them are often at odds with each other. Jim and Jen could feel the tension growing and their control over their family life diminishing. The world was seeping into their familial relationships like rainwater through a porous foundation after a soaking, late-winter rain.

ADJUSTMENT, COMPROMISE, SELF-DOUBT

The elementary school in their new neighborhood is a handsome brick structure firmly perched halfway up a sloping hill with playing fields below and a playground above. The school is safe and orderly. The principal and teachers are conscientious. Test scores are high relative to other public schools. The Parents Association is well-funded and exhibits the good taste to invest in arts programs for the children. The productions that result from these programs are impressive. But as a public school, it is limited in what it can do, and the quality of teacher a child receives from year to year is random. When Suzie first entered the school, she had a significant adjustment to make inasmuch she was placed in a class with an authoritarian teacher who simply delivered information and directives to students who were struggling to sit quietly in their seats. Unlike the ECC, the teacher was not interested in working through the children's ideas with them or in adjusting the curriculum to cultivate their interests into a passion. Suzie had to learn to keep her ideas to herself and speak only in response to the teacher's requests for information. After a few months she made the adjustment and over the course of several years adapted all too well as she recognized that she could get the highest grades and skate through school by simply performing menial homework and in-school assignments efficiently and with a smile. By the middle of her third year in the school, the love of learning that had animated her at the ECC had been diluted and diminished by the public school curriculum, which is built around the insistence that students perform well on standardized tests. As Jim and Jen had feared, the education their daughters would get in the public school was but a shadow of what it could be.

As they thought about their situation, they came to see that they too were adjusting to their new situation in more ways than they had anticipated. It appeared that just as the community among parents reflected the community of children in the school at the ECC, the relationships in their new community also reflected the community surrounding the school. The school's primary focus is on results, the outcomes of test scores, rather than on cultivating a passion for the process of learning. Likewise, parents, for the most part, are focused on results such as in the monetary results of their careers and the goods they can purchase, rather than on the quality of their lives as lived each day. And even though Jim was not primarily interested in being a money-maker, he found himself deferring to and overly respecting many of his neighbors who were successful wage-earners. In fact, like Steve Shannon, whom we met in the previous chapter, the more time Jim spent around his neighbors, the more he wrestled with his own career choice. He often found himself questioning whether or not they had it right and that there was nothing more important than gaining as much spending power as possible. Maybe, he thought, he should change careers in order to earn more money so that he could buy a larger house for his family and relieve some of the stress that developed between Jen and him as their taxes and expenses continued to increase more quickly than their income.

Beyond his career, Jim found himself doubting things he once felt so strongly about. At a neighbor's barbecue, for instance, he inexplicably accepted an offer to eat a hamburger after he had enjoyed fourteen years of vegetarianism. He began to question the importance he had placed on education after witnessing first-hand the lack of quality in the education some of his colleagues at the college were offering. In his darker moments, Jim speculated that his neighbors, who earned so much money, were the real men and that his life as a music teacher was too sheltered. Maybe he needed to show his mettle by competing in the world of business and commerce.

These dark moments became even darker when he began to suspect, privately, that Jen sometimes felt the same way. The self-doubt Jim periodically hoisted onto himself became almost unbearable when he sensed that Jen doubted him as well. With depleted self-confidence, he even wondered if it was selfish of him to pursue an academic career that didn't pay as well as other professions. His salary, even along with the income generated from giving private lessons, seemed paltry next to the enormous houses, Range Rovers, and swimming pools of his neighbors. In these moments of uncertainty, Jim felt alone as he went through the routines of parenting his children.

RECOVERING THE SELF IN QUIET COMMUNITIES

It was during these times that he most looked forward to bringing his daughters to their music lessons three nights a week. On the back porch of the school building, listening through half-opened windows to abbreviated pieces of Bach and Beethoven, Mozart and Liszt, pieced together on the undersized instruments of children, he could read and think in peace and with purpose. Here he was able to recover a sense of self by sitting on the periphery of a different community, a musical community that stretched back centuries and was now being carried forth in the generational exchange between teacher and student inside the school.

It was on the porch that he also took his place in the ancient community of literary and philosophical minds springing to life in the pages of the texts he held on his lap to read. With these more abstract but no less influential communities of music and books to support him, a dimension of Jim's life that felt under assault in the surroundings of his home came back to life. On the porch of his daughter's music school he could address the tensions of his place and his role in his community with broader insight and stronger conviction. He noticed that he felt more alive on the porch, in tune with who he wanted to be. Words and ideas emanating from texts resonated with him deeply and animated him in a way that nothing else could. From the porch, he could see the merits and joys of his life as an educator and artist, along with its limitations. He also found a degree of clarity with which he could assess the merits and limitations of those among whom he lived and whose lifestyle caused him to feel so much self-doubt.

Against the backdrop of a school of teachers that nurtured budding musicians, he was reminded of the importance of what he was doing as a teacher and as a musician. He remembered that education means something very different to him than it does to most of his neighbors. He knows that the local public school's emphasis on standardized tests as a measure of student achievement is usually antithetical to real learning, as is the mind-set of parents who are overly concerned with such results because they might someday have an effect on the college their children will attend. These misplaced concerns become all too evident in the stories that surface, year after year, of parents who do their children's homework, argue with teachers about how their child should be given more attention, or negotiate with the principal about special placement for their son or daughter. Jim also recalled that this same mentality spreads well beyond the schools. Year after year there are stories of parents who manipulate the selection process of softball and soccer teams by holding the façade of tryouts, and then placing their friend's children on teams regardless of ability. One particular night, before leaving these thoughts to return to his book, he bolstered his sense of priorities and self further when he replayed in his mind the shocking episode that followed a conversation with his neighbor a week earlier.

Jim had just finished cutting his grass when his neighbor, Joe, crossed the street to offer him tickets to the Mets game the following night. Jim wasn't interested in going to the game and politely declined, but the conversation moved on to grass-cutting, the weather, and, more abstractly, to the future. Joe mentioned that he admired the way Jim seemed to take time to "smell the flowers," pointing out that he regularly spotted

Jim standing quietly in his yard, seemingly lost in thought. "I need to slow down and do more of that," Joe continued. "My problem is that I measure my worth as a man by how much I earn. I know that sounds pathetic, but it's true. You don't seem to have the same way of thinking." Jim was slightly taken back by the directness of Joe's confession, though not completely surprised. "Money is important," Jim responded, not wanting to get into a protracted conversation about the meaning and purpose of money and, ultimately, life. "But I guess there are other things I'm interested in." Joe quickly sensed that Jim was evading the conversation and gently ended it by saying, "Let me know if you change your mind about the tickets," as he turned to walk back to his house.

The next morning, shortly before six, eleven FBI cars surrounded Joe's house. They knocked on his door with rifles ready. Upon opening the door, he was ordered to stay where he was. Only his wife could go upstairs to get him clothes so that he could dress himself. The agents did not even allow him to say goodbye to his two young children before they handcuffed him and escorted him into the back of a car. He spent the next several days in prison and the following months under house arrest.

According to the newspaper, Joe used his status as an attorney to visit with a convicted mob boss in prison and carry his orders about whom to murder to people on the outside. His conversations were taped. Upon reading the story, the conversation Jim had with Joe the night before his arrest took on added significance. Joe was serious about how he measured his worth as a man. He valued the acquisition of wealth so much that he was willing to gamble everything else in his life: his career, his family, his reputation—and he lost.

Jim and Jen spent the next several days responding to their daughter's questions about what had occurred to her friend's dad. Silently, they were contemplating just how different their lives as parents were now compared with the early years of parenting. Their community had grown and, with greater complexity and size, their influence over their lives and the lives of their children was diminished. Their children had been playing in the yard of a man whom federal authorities had deemed so threatening that they sent eleven cars of armed men to arrest him and bring him to prison.

Jim had intuitively sensed shortcomings in his neighbor and avoided substantial conversations with him. And while it is not difficult to distinguish oneself from such behaviors in the community, the influence of community is usually much more subtle than that of neighbors who get caught on the wrong side of the law. There are ever-present influences that penetrate our homes and minds through the conversations we have, through the television, the computer, video games, and ill-timed visits from the ice cream truck. The ability to chart out an ideally balanced, nutritional meal plan for the family seemed like a fading memory of a different kind of life to Jen as she considered her place in her new community.

The goals and values we hold in our minds at the beginning of the parenting journey seem to be under constant siege as we navigate the unpredictable tides of community life, forcing us to revise and sometimes even abandon them. We deny our children access to video games or junk food in the home, only to find that these are precisely the attractions they gravitate to at a neighbor's house. We sign them up for athletic teams only to discover they are in chat rooms with the older teammates, being exposed to the world of boyfriends or girlfriends for the first time and well before their time. We limit their time in front of the television, only to learn that they are left out of conversations when they go to school and ridiculed when they do not know the shows their classmates are talking about.

In the early years of caring for an infant, we have the ability to decide who they interact with and what we will expose children to. As their world grows more complex, that power gets dispersed. Our communities are only partially of our choosing. The communities in which we find ourselves have an established sensibility or culture of their own embedded in them. The community sets the agenda and generates the issues we will wrestle with. Living in communities with children, our families being the primary community, we realize that it is a constant struggle to know where we stand or to identify and live by the principles in which we believe. The self seems to be constantly under siege as if there were no resting place to find some peace, to know who one really is.

COMMUNITY IN SELF

One lesson we learn from the story of Jim and Jen is that we are embedded in communities, and those communities challenge us to constantly update our understanding of who we are as individuals and as families. Given the pervasiveness of conflicting community values that we face, we often long for an escape to a solitary place, a private world that does not let the outside world in. But very often this longing is generated from a misunderstanding of the relationship between self and community. Communities are embedded in us just as much as we are embedded in communities. We do not escape communities, not even in solitude. Jim learned this on the porch of his child's school. By getting outside of one community that was undermining his sense of self, he was able to participate in a very different type of community that supported what he valued. In solitude, a state that parents do well to experience from time to time, we are not alone. We simply switch communities rather than leaving them behind. To understand that we can never completely escape community is an important step for parents to make in overcoming a major source of frustration. To suggest that community is embedded in us, just as we are embedded in community, is another way of saying that there is no "I," no self, without community. Unfortunately, this is a lesson that is widely missed in American culture today. In fact, this idea seems to be at odds with so much of what we value and cherish.

THE DECLINE OF INDIVIDUALISM

Individualism and self-reliance are central to the American identity. This sentiment is captured with forceful eloquence in "Self-Reliance"— Emerson's seminal essay—that gave voice to these ideals of adulthood during our nation's infancy. He emphasizes the virtue of trusting in and developing oneself: "What I must do is all that concerns me, not what the people think. This rule . . . may serve for the whole distinction between greatness and meanness."[1] The great man does not look to authority or tradition for justification or support, nor does he take cues from society to guide him toward greatness. In fact, Emerson sees society as a conspiracy "against the manhood of every one of its members."[2] In contrast, the great man is "he who in the midst of the crowd keeps with perfect sweetness the independence of solitude."[3]

The ideology of individualism that Emerson champions early in our nation's history has led to leaps of ingenuity and accomplishment, as well as shaped the expectations and culture of the American family. The most pervasive example of this expectation, perhaps, is the rite of passage that most teenagers go through in leaving the home for college or work. Stepping out on one's own is an expectation that is built into the very fabric of the American psyche and continues throughout adulthood, as our respect for the "self-made man" clearly shows. Not only is the timeline of departure from the home embedded into the consciousness of parents, it also informs major plans for entire families.

But the individualism that Emerson emphasized has gone astray in contemporary society. Self-reliance is by no means the same as selfishness, while selfishness has become the preeminent value that drives American culture. A closer look at Emerson's essay reveals that the title, "Self-Reliance," is, at first glance, somewhat misleading. Emerson certainly did insist that individuals assume responsibility for their lives and look within to find greatness rather than without, but the turn inward leads to more than a mere egoistic individual. A careful and sustained turn inward opens out into the light of the divine. Greatness is possible for us, not because we are great on our own, but because we are animated by a "divine spark" uniquely suited to each of us: "The eye was placed where one ray should fall, that it might testify of that particular ray."[4]

The measure of human greatness transcends the individual by finding a place in nature that, for Emerson, embodies the divine. For him, to take control of one's life involves receiving the intelligence of nature or the divine in our own unique way. In solitude, we perceive the spark of wisdom and insight and recognize that we are—that we live—in a relationship with the common cause of everything. It is in this common origin that we find the measure of greatness and the source of strength required to achieve it. The individual, therefore, is never really solitary. He is independent of social convention but dependent on nature, the divine, or both. It is precisely his independence that enables him to enter into an interdependent community that articulates higher goods and standards. While Emerson's individualism has led to much greatness over the course of our history, it has become detached from its proper measure. With this detachment, a truncated form of individualism has taken over and feeds an accelerating deterioration of American society. Individualism without restraint is selfishness that acts like a cancer eating away at the common good.

The obvious symptoms of selfish individualism and the corrosion of the common good are found in the ongoing saga of a deteriorating middle class where anxiety dominates the lives of parents. As Jim and Jen were slowly discovering, a middle-class income is no match for the escalating cost of health care, education, and energy. While job security, retirement security, and access to health care decline, anxiety rises, an anxiety that saps the motivation to contribute to the common good of society. Rather than practicing this kind of commitment, parents are forced to focus on procuring the material needs of their families regardless of what happens to the common good.

As I write this chapter, we are experiencing wide-scale consequences of selfish individualism as the Federal Reserve scrambles to save the economy from a financial meltdown. Bear Stearns, a prestigious investment bank worth more than $150 a share a little more than a year ago, was sold for $2 a share in an emergency bailout. This collapse, one among many others, is the result of bankers, mortgage brokers, and consumers overreaching to make imprudent financial deals driven by greed of one sort or another. Whether selling or buying unaffordable loans, they have transformed the American concern with the common good into the pursuit of their own personal good. The hyper-consumerism that has gripped the American psyche for so many years sees what is left of the common good and community as mere fodder for their greed.

But selfish individualism is not limited to Wall Street inasmuch as it permeates the minds of too many Americans and is in fact most striking when it arises in roles that were previously reserved for those dedicated to the common good. I stopped attending youth basketball games in my community because I found it too painful to watch coaches who were interested only in the well-being of their own children. In a scene familiar to many parents, there was one overanimated coach who was only interested in the girls on the team insofar as they could help his daughter succeed as an individual. When his daughter was in the game, he coached incessantly, intent on telling them where to go and when to pass to his daughter. On the rare occasion his daughter was not in the game, he virtually stopped coaching. He let the girls run up and down the court while he looked at the clock to see when he could put his daughter back in the game.

This simple but sad example of selfish disregard for the common good of a youth sports team is by no means an isolated occurrence. The mentality is widespread. Some are better at disguising it than others. Wherever it exists, however, it demonstrates a gross misunderstanding of our place in community as well as the ways in which self and community rise and fall together. This coach, like greedy bankers and legislators who make rules to facilitate their greed, fail to understand that human nature is at its core communal. To pursue selfish goals with contempt for the common good is to act against our own nature. It is to forget that the more we contribute to our community, the more we benefit as individuals.

The tension between individualism and commitment to community is felt most powerfully by parents, who are concerned about far more than bad business practices and their consequences. The deeper lesson is that good as well as bad values shape our communities and, sometimes, our most important decisions. These values not only affect the way we live now, but are indeed transmitted to our children simply by the way we model them. Selfishness will never satisfy any human being. It closes us off from the divine spark that Emerson's ideal self relies on as well as from the communities that sustain it. It is those who are animated by that divine spark and fan it with the flame of commitment to the common good that find real satisfaction.

ENDURING COMMUNITIES

Family is the first community in which children live and begin to forge an identity, and it is family that leaves an indelible influence on each of its members. Before James joined his friends in cheering for the Mets, he had already assimilated ways of dealing with community by participating in his own family community. In the very act of rooting for different teams, we enjoy a community formed around a general interest in sports. By respecting James's choice, we help form a space in which his interests are free to emerge. To watch and listen to him express such interests is one of our great privileges and joys. My concern as his father is not about which team he roots for; it is, rather, in his ability to trust in his choices, express them with increasing clarity and confidence, and to participate fully in community. These practices and the values on which they are based form our original community. And I suspect that it is these practices and values that stay with us for life. In doing so, they provide us with an orientation to approach and negotiate all kinds of communities.

To say that we are communal is to say that we are always engaged in conversation with someone or something. If not conversing with a live person, we are engaged in dialogue with a memory, an idea, or an aspiration. Who we are at any given moment is shaped and informed by the memories of the past and the ideals for the future. The idea that we are fully contained, fully realized individuals at any given moment is a relic of a misinformed past. The self is embedded in and shaped by communities, and communities are embedded in the self.

INNER COMMUNITIES

Sometimes the communities that influence us the most are made up of voices from our past, and it is precisely these communities that are carried forward from the past in the inner recesses of the mind to shape the present. I was reminded of an inner community formed out of my past last summer when I set out to build a porch on the side of my house. I learned how to build over many years working with my father and brother. It is rewarding to look back on those years, the work we did, and the skills we acquired. But there were also many tense days on those jobs filled with anger and frustration. One of the prime sources of frustration on those jobs was the command that came from my father to get food, tea, or coffee for any and all subcontractors who worked for us. These men did not expect this service because they never received it on any of their other jobs. Yet when they worked for us, we were required to be at their service, regardless of what we were doing. At the time, the command to get food for these strangers felt demeaning. It wasn't that I didn't want them to have it, or even that I didn't want to get it for them; I just didn't want to be told to stop whatever I was doing to get it for them.

I planned the porch for several weeks, drawing plans, estimating materials, and figuring the best time to start. Night after night I thought through each step of the process from cutting the rafters to the method I would use to lift and fasten them by myself. I measured repeatedly, marked my lines and built the partitions. When I had the walls up and the roof on, I arranged for Jerry, the plasterer, to do the stucco. I enjoyed making this arrangement because I knew Jerry and his work. It would be easy to make a fair deal with him, and I found it satisfying to not only build but to bring competent help onto the job when I needed it.

Jerry came by to see the job. We ironed out some details and two days later, while I was at work, he arrived with his crew of five men. They blasted through the day, getting it prepared for the first coat of stucco. They had a commitment the following day, however, so Jerry asked if they could work on Sunday. There would be little noise so I was confident my neighbors wouldn't mind. I was waiting for his crew when they arrived at 7:30 and let them into the garage where their tools were stored. They wasted no time moving to their stations, some on a scaffold, others on the ground. When their work was underway, I walked around the front of my house to pick up the Sunday newspaper and went inside to read. I pulled the paper from its blue plastic package but before sitting something pulled me into the kitchen, where I found a pencil and paper. Leaving the newspaper behind, I went outside and stood beneath the crew leader who was working on the scaffold. "Amigo," I shouted. "What can I get you and your men for breakfast?"

Looking back on that job, it became clear to me that we are always in conversation and community, sometimes with our contemporaries and sometimes with voices from our past. Since I learned to build from my father, it is his voice that speaks when I build now. He too would spend hours each evening planning and rehearsing a job in his head. And the practice of getting food for other workers that frustrated me as a teenager became the natural thing for me to do now. In working with my father, I not only learned how to build; I also acquired an appreciation for the hardship and integrity of workers. These are values, it turns out, that shaped the community of our family and became an integral part of how, today, I relate to others.

This is what we give to our children, values that demonstrate our commitments and determine the way our communities are held together. While there was a part of me that would have enjoyed putting my feet up and losing myself in the Sunday news, the attraction to serve those men, who came from a different world and spoke a different language, was stronger. As I drove to the deli to get their breakfast, I had a rewarding sense of camaraderie with them and with my father.

OUR COMMUNAL NATURE

To some this story might seem like little more than the acting out of psychological baggage held over from my youth. In *The Drama of the Gifted Child,* psychologist Alice Miller makes painfully clear the damage inflicted on children by parents who fail to understand their own emotional wounds suffered in their youth.[5] She shows clearly the need to break cycles of unconscious behavior that inflict the unresolved hurt and suffering of parents onto their children. But we should be careful not to equate these harmful cycles with positive influences from our past that inform who we are and enable us to take a stand in the world. It is by listening to and understanding the different and at times conflicting voices of past communities, in particular the community of family, that shapes who we are.

Inasmuch as we are never free of community influences, whether from the present, past, or future, whether in a crowd or all alone, it is critically important to understand them and not to forget they not only exist but do, moreover, persist. The selfish individualism that pervades American society asks us to act in opposition to our communal, dialogical nature. From the very beginning, in the womb, we are engaged in an interdependent, reciprocal relationship. Although the circumstances of our relationships change as we grow and become more self-reliant, reciprocity and interdependence do indeed remain. To overlook the indelible influence of community in shaping who we are is to misunderstand who we are, and this, in turn, makes it very difficult to know our place in the world. To misunderstand the formative forces of the self is to be held captive by them and when we are so held captive, we are sure to inflict their negative influences on our children. On the other hand, to acknowledge and hear them gives us an opportunity to know who we are and who we want to become.

As parents, we direct much of our attention to shaping and controlling the communities in which our children grow and develop. We not only participate in communities of the present—communities of work, religion, school, or sports—but are also informed and shaped by more subtle, less noticeable communities that span the future and the past. We discover early on that the demands and influences of communities outside the family are often at odds with those within the family. Sometimes your son will root for the rival of your favorite team. Later on, he may choose a group of friends you don't approve of or a career path that you know will be a lifelong struggle. We cannot take these choices away from growing children, but the way they approach their choices will depend in large part on how we allow them to participate in the family community. The team that my seven-year-old roots for is not important. The fact that we can share an interest, that he can express his interests and be heard, that he is free to explore a deepening interest and share what he finds makes him an essential part of our family community.

Our understanding of communities and the way we relate to them therefore represents a critical turning point in the lives of families. Community is central to our identity as parents, to the identity of our children, and the identity of families. This chapter is placed at the center of this book intentionally because, to the extent that we achieve any of the other turning points, we do so in communities. Community, then, is more than simply one turning point among others; it is the turning point in which the ability of parents to grow up by working through the other turning points is demonstrated—or not.

5

GRATITUDE

To suggest that gratitude is an essential virtue for the well-being of parents may be out of step with how many of us feel as we struggle to meet the mounting challenges of raising children today. We worry about their health and safety while struggling to keep pace with mounting bills. We fumble about for the right words to console hurt feelings, often missing the mark. We sacrifice our social lives to save for exorbitant college tuition bills. We honor their birthdays with parties, performances in a school play with flowers, and a good report card with gifts. We spend time and money supporting their sports teams, music lessons, vacations, and camps. Throw in the emotional energy required to handle relationships with growing children and adolescents who seem destined to rebel and resist, and there is little time, it seems, for feeling gratitude.

To make things more difficult, gratitude is rarely the first response of children to what they have or what their parents do. In our weaker moments, we sometimes resent their selfishness and wonder why we sacrifice so much for what they don't seem to want. During these times, gratitude seems like a far-off dream, absent from the emerging personalities of our children and from our own lives. And yet I am suggesting that gratitude is one of the most essential virtues for parents, not only to effectively raise children but also to live a full life. Without gratitude, life never rises above the strain and struggle of household battles. Without gratitude, life is absent of joy. Holocaust survivor Elie Wiesel suggests that a person without gratitude is missing something in his or her humanity.

As with all of the virtues that are essential for living a good life, parents are faced with the double task of cultivating gratitude in themselves and nurturing it in their children. Because parents face so many obstacles in finding gratitude, we tend to overlook its importance. But we overlook it at great peril because it is, according to Cicero, not only the greatest of virtues, but the parent of all virtue.

Gratitude makes the other virtues possible. One who is grateful for the gift of life is more likely to show compassion to others. One who is grateful for those upon whom his life depends can more easily see a common humanity in the downtrodden and can more easily fight for justice. Those who understand the fragility of life and are grateful for their own can see the importance of temperance in a world of excess. To the extent that we want to give our children an opportunity to live their lives to the fullest, we have an obligation to sew in them the seeds of thankfulness. To neglect this obligation is to deny them the possibility of achieving an excellence of human character, an essential element of their humanity, and the possibility of achieving what they are capable of.

As we will discover in this chapter, gratitude is unique among the virtues. Not only is it a prerequisite to the other virtues, it is the most pleasing of virtues, a primal source of joy that transforms our experience of the world when we find it. William Blake went so far as to describe gratitude as "heaven itself." To be grateful is to share the joy that one feels as a result of having received something pleasing. And this desire to share is itself joyful. So gratitude is joy compounded—a pleasure on top of a pleasure. For parents, this joy can be a source of strength to aid us in meeting the challenges of everyday life. To experience it, however, parents must first know where to look for it.

GRATITUDE FROM THE GUIDANCE OF A CHILD

Jack and Rose were saddened and frustrated when their son was diagnosed with a particularly stubborn learning disorder that not only im-

paired his ability to learn in school but made social adaptation difficult
as well. Dennis's physical development is normal, and so his unorthodox
responses take people by surprise when they first meet him. Jack and
Rose spent years searching for a school that would help Dennis, but
their search came up empty after several tries that were punctuated
with trauma each time he switched schools. Jack and Rose were both
highly successful professionals, though Rose had already taken a break
from work to handle the daily grind of raising two children, one with
special needs. Jack was a leading New York physician with a flourishing
practice that demanded long hours. He had the financial resources to
find the best care for Dennis, but the hours and the time away from his
family were getting to him. He was frustrated with the inability to find a
school that could help Dennis, and there was little social support in his
suburban community.

In examining the circumstances of their lives, Jack and Rose found
themselves questioning their entire lifestyle: the commute, the hours,
the taxes. Questions about lifestyle led to more philosophical questions
such as, "What is the best way to live?" and "What is the purpose of life
in general?" They didn't come up with a specific answer to the latter,
but an answer to the former came into focus over the course of several
months of conversations. Jack was indeed tired of the grind and felt
that there was more that he wanted to do with his life, beginning with
spending more time with Dennis and teaching him what he could. This
could be done best in a completely different setting, he thought, where
there was space, natural beauty, and a slower pace of life. Jack and
Rose became convinced that their future would be best lived out in the
country where they would grow their own food and teach their children
to do the same. They would care for animals that their children would
befriend and love. Rose would take up sewing again, a latent passion of
hers, and teach the craft to her daughter.

A few years into their new life, they found a peace and joy they weren't
sure was possible before they tried. Although they didn't consciously
make it a policy, each meal in their house begins with a small grace, a
heartfelt expression of their gratitude for each other, for their home that
keeps them warm and dry, for their food, their animal friends, and the
beauty and diversity of nature; privately, Jack and Rose would offer a
prayer of gratitude for Dennis.

Their new life has ushered their thinking and concerns beyond the inevitable comparisons with other children and families that arose shortly after Dennis's problems emerged. They are grateful for what they have and unconcerned about what they do not have. They are grateful to Dennis for showing them the way. In responding to the call that came from his unique life, they found the path they wanted for themselves and for their family. In accepting Dennis as he is and responding to their love for him, they discovered a new world made up of a different network of people, slower rhythms to the day, brighter concerns and conversations, and new aspirations for themselves and their children. They are no longer frustrated that Dennis won't go to a top college; they are grateful he is caring for their vegetables and their horse with a smile that was absent for years in unsuitable and inhospitable schools.

By having the courage to look beneath the surface of Dennis's life, Jack and Rose found a unique gift that others could not see: the gift of a son who did not fit into the mainstream led them to find the gift of a new life for the whole family. Each night when they offer a prayer of thanks, Jack and Rose feel a deep satisfaction with life that was absent in the city. This fullness reinforces their strength and confirms the decision they made to change course. It is this fullness that makes gratitude unique because, like love, it needs to be shared. Unlike a debt that carries an obligation to be paid, gratitude is never a burden: it is an effusive expression of joy. In *The Ethics*, Spinoza defines gratitude as "the desire, or eagerness of love, whereby we endeavor to benefit one who from a like emotion of love, has bestowed benefit on us."[1] Love in this case is another word for the fullness that compels us to offer good will and thankfulness to the other. This fullness makes gratitude the opposite of selfishness, which is driven by an emptiness that is seeking to be filled. The ungrateful or selfish person always needs more. He cannot see what there is to be grateful for and, hence, never has enough. Gratitude is the awareness and recognition of what one has already received and is happy with.

Jack and Rose demonstrate that gratitude can be found in response to the most difficult circumstances and lead to a transcendence of social expectations and norms that often constrain the human spirit. They also show that gratitude is not just a fleeting gesture like a spark of light that does little to illuminate a dark room. To become grateful can be a dramatic turning point for parents insofar as it redirects our vision and the focus of our concerns: to be grateful is to see the world in a different way. This vision looks carefully at things, especially the ones we ordinarily take for granted. Sometimes it is our children themselves whom we take for granted and sometimes it is the things we do for them, like throwing a birthday party. To the critic and the crank, these are silly practices, a waste of time and resources that send our children the wrong message about what is and is not important. But looked at from a different point of view, even a birthday party can evoke a sense of gratitude. In fact, in some ways, a birthday party is an expression of gratitude.

A Birthday Celebration

I mention looking beneath the surface of birthday parties because most of the time I am the one who criticizes them as frivolous exercises of excess that breed the antithesis of gratitude in our children. A seven-year-old's birthday party now requires a rented gym or restaurant along with live entertainment. An entire roster of classmates is invited, each one arriving with the compulsory present that his parents darted to the store to buy the day before. At the end of the party, at which food is ordered to arrive just after the clown finishes performing, the birthday boy sits down to begin tearing feverishly through presents, leaving mounds of wrapping paper to the side. He glances momentarily at each one, occasionally expressing a mild satisfaction before moving on the next. The pace is fast and furious; he hardly has time to look up and say "Thank you." These are not gifts in the real sense. They are obligatory tokens of membership, a minimal fee to justify one's presence at the party. And just like Christmas, the biggest birthday celebration of all, the intent of the party is lost beneath the mound of wasted paper and plastic toys. For many years, this discouraging portrait of birthday celebrations reinforced an instinctual aversion I've held toward them since childhood. And this aversion kept me from giving much thought to birthday celebrations until I had my eyes opened to what they can mean when approached in a different way.

Getting Help to Celebrate a Birthday

In the late summer of 2004, I broke a private rule I held for myself and my children. The rule was that neither they nor I would miss school or work strictly for pleasure. But at the end of the summer, I decided I would take a couple of days off from teaching, and have my seven-year-old daughter, Caitriona, miss the first few days of third grade in order to travel to Ireland to watch the All-Ireland hurling final in Dublin. Over the years, I had become friends with D.J. Carey, who is widely regarded as the best player in the history of the sport. He was coming to the end of his career and his team was playing for its third All-Ireland victory in a row, which hadn't been done by any team since the 1970s. I thought it would be worth it for my daughter to experience the All-Ireland final weekend while we knew someone who was directly involved. And we could spend her eighth birthday together the day after the game.

The morning of the game we woke early to drive to Dublin before the traffic built-up. We arrived at D.J.'s house much earlier than expected, however, and when I knocked on the door, I woke up the house. D.J. answered the door in his bathrobe and welcomed us in but since it was too early I decided to drive around the neighborhood I had lived in for a year when I was a student at University College Dublin. Along the way, I pointed out various landmarks such as the apartment I lived in, the field I ran on, and the hill I frequently climbed. Each sight evoked a polite but unenthused "cool" from my daughter. When it no longer felt intrusive, we returned to D.J.'s house where Sarah, his fiancée, guests, and children were wide awake with excitement. His children took my daughter to play in the back while the adults had breakfast. When we finished eating, D.J. invited me to walk with him to the bay, where he soaked his legs before each game. He told me it had something to do with the iodine in the water and that this helped him avoid injuries.

Our walk to and from the bay was my first up-close experience of celebrity. D.J. politely greeted old and young as they wished him good luck in the All-Ireland. Mothers ran from strollers, abandoning children inside in order to shake his hand or simply get a closer glimpse. As we walked back from the bay on a sidewalk wide enough for only one person, D.J. calmly turned to me and said, "Watch this one." He had noticed a car driving past with Cork flags and jerseys, the colors of the team he would be opposing later in the day. I looked up in time to see the car swerve recklessly onto the sidewalk ahead of us. Two boys jumped out with pen and paper in hand running toward D.J. As they got closer, their legs slowed down while their eyes and mouths opened wide, though they were unable to speak. D.J. helped them out casually asking, "How're ye lads?" He took the pen and paper from the smaller of the two. "What's your name?" "Shane," he responded. "Good lad, Shane. Here you are," D.J. said, as he handed the paper back with an inscription personalized to Shane above his signature. He did the same for Michael, the older of the two boys. They both managed to say "Thank you very much, D.J." I could almost feel the lightness in their steps as they bounced back to their father's car.

The Dublin sky was a familiar charcoal-grey dropping an intermittent mist before the game. My daughter fell asleep in her seat just before the game started, but woke with the roar of the crowd after the first score. I was tired and found myself focusing on D.J. rather than the game as a whole, and it seemed as if he was being given a lot of space by his defender. Ten minutes into the game, it looked as if his chance to electrify the crowd and his team had come. With his characteristic blast of speed, he darted toward the goal where the ball had broken free. The crowd rose with an anticipation that only D.J. could stir among 80,000 people as he zeroed in on the ball with the goal straight ahead. He was unstoppable once he had the ball on the run, and, when he scored, it lifted his team and all of their supporters like no other athlete I have ever seen. But just as he was about to take the ball onto his stick, a teammate crossed in front of him, lifted the ball, and hit it wide of the goal. The stadium and his team were deflated. They seemed to lose their edge after that play and with it their chance at a third All-Ireland in a row.

D.J.'s father, John, invited us to the players' reception after the game. I felt slightly awkward about being among the losing team and with D.J., not knowing how he would take the loss. Although he was disappointed, he remained pleasant and courteous as he congratulated an opponent in the elevator that was carrying us down from the reception. Outside the stadium he joked about some of the sights of disheveled fans, and on the trip back to the house we managed to avoid talking about the game.

Later that night, D.J. invited me to a team reception at a large hotel. Outside the hotel bar there was an overflow of fans from the game.

Security opened a private passage way for him to avoid the crowd. Inside there was the usual hotel-style reception, speeches, a preheated salmon or steak dinner, and young people drinking lots of beer. The night was uneventful, for the most part, until fans in the overcrowded bar spotted D.J. leaving. Several immediately swarmed around him, including some from the opposing team who had drunk themselves almost legless. Verging on incoherence, they began slobbering their amateur analysis of the game to D.J., who stood patiently, listening and responding to the drunkards with the same respect he gave to the children who asked for autographs and to everyone else who crossed his path that day. I was in awe of his calmness and composure as well as his ability to tolerate frivolity, even in the midst of great disappointment.

The next morning I woke with my daughter. I wished her a happy birthday as we waited for the others to wake. The children came down first and D.J. followed shortly after. He played with the children for a few minutes before falling onto a large couch. "How are you feeling?" was a loaded question the day after one loses a bid to win a third All-Ireland final in a row in what might have been the final game of his career. But I asked nonetheless. "Not too bad," he responded, his voice slightly softer than usual. "I got a few belts." That was the most I ever heard him say about getting hit on a hurling field, though I know he often did, so I suspected the hits he took were significant. "Where did you get hit?" I asked. He rolled up the leg of his pants to show me the deepest, most colorful bruise I had ever seen, a perfectly shaped replica of the hurling stick, literally in the flesh. "Ahh, I heal quickly," he said.

When Sarah came into the room, the conversation shifted to what we would do with the kids for the morning before the team train traveled back to Kilkenny for a city-wide reception in the center of town. She had family and friends visiting from England and we all easily agreed to take the children for a walk by the sea. We strolled casually along the cement walkway above the heavy sand, conversations shifting smoothly from topic to topic and person to person. As we turned back toward the house, D.J. pointed out the makeshift tents along the strand that served as meeting posts for the homosexual community of Dublin, a stark contrast to the million-dollar homes perched above.

Rather than simply doubling back to retrace our steps, however, we took a slight left onto a street lined with old buildings rising from below the grade to our right. D.J. and Sarah walked ahead and dipped down a short set of stairs, gesturing for us to follow. It was an old-style pub with low tables spaciously placed around the bar. We took seats as Sarah talked to one of the waitresses. The adults ordered tea or coffee with Irish bread and soup. But before any of the food came, the waitress arrived holding a cake with eight candles aflame on top. She placed it in front of my daughter while a group of adults and children, most of whom we had met for the first time the previous day, sang "Happy Birthday." My daughter was fighting back tears because, at that moment, she missed her mother, her sister, and her brother, and I was moved by a profound sense of gratitude and admiration for the selfless awareness of D.J. and Sarah, who, in the midst of momentous events and disappointment and with guests and children of their own to care for, remembered and took the time to recognize my daughter's birthday. When my daughter saw the other children having fun in her honor, and bit into her first piece of cake, she quickly overcame her loneliness.

We left the restaurant and headed back to the house. D.J., Sarah, and their children would travel on the team train to Kilkenny, while Caitriona and I would drive ahead and join the crowd in welcoming them. Or so I thought. They had already arranged to have Caitriona travel with them on the team train. I drove back on my own and met with D.J.'s father who took me to the train station where the team would arrive, along with my daughter. "They'll be here in a few minutes and we'll get on that bus," he said, as he pointed to a topless double-decker parked a few yards away. The bus he was referring to was the team bus that would ride through narrow medieval streets of the city lined with tens of thousands of people cheering for their heroes. As the bus twisted slowly through the crowd, I laughed as young women held up signs offering themselves in marriage to players sitting behind me. Leather-skinned men, including some former All-Ireland champions, blended into the crowd, gesturing approving glances from under their caps.

After slowly winding our way through the town, we arrived in a large parking lot where a stage had been constructed to introduce the team to the crowd. As with all teams, some players were more popular than others and I privately looked forward to hearing the reception D.J. would receive for his years of greatness. One by one, the players lumbered across the stage, weighed down by defeat and a night of drinking. Then D.J. was called. Expectedly, the crowd roared louder than before. Unlike his teammates, D.J. faced the crowd as he walked and returned the cheer by clapping toward them, a sign of appreciation for their cheers.

On the surface, it is easy to be grateful for being treated so well by our hosts. To have access to the inside workings of an athlete and a sport at the highest level, on its most important day, was such an extraordinary thrill that it justified breaking the private rule of not missing work or school for pleasure. The magnanimity of our hosts, however, revealed something much more enduring about gratitude than what I felt in response to their hospitality. Their hospitality forced me to reflect on the significance of honoring birthdays.

As I thought about the simple but moving birthday party they spontaneously organized in honor of my daughter, there was no place for the usual objections I held against parties. On the contrary, their gesture led me to think carefully about specific events and moments from my daughter's life during the two-hour drive from Dublin to Kilkenny. The more I thought about these events, the simpler they became until I found myself smiling in response to my image of her smiling. When I thought of her laughing, I felt my gut filling with joy. And as I held the image of her smiling face in my mind, I zeroed in on the quirky way she moves her nose from time to time. At that moment, in response to that simple image, I couldn't imagine anything more special. I was full of gratitude for her life as I remembered a line from Albert Schweitzer, who said that we each have cause to think with deep gratitude of those who have lighted the flame within us. This, I learned, is why we celebrate the birthdays of family and friends: to honor and thank the people who light our flame to live and work, to play and pray. Beneath the wrapping papers, boxes, and clowns, there is a message of thanks being offered to our children for being who they are. And if our "thank you" is sincere, it is far more than a momentary expression: it is what Meister Eckhart, the great Christian mystic, called a prayer. If "thank you" is the only prayer we ever said, he assures us, it would suffice. I never before imagined a birthday party as a prayer, but now I do.

THE CHALLENGES OF CULTIVATING GRATITUDE

Jack and Rose found gratitude through their courage to follow the direction their son's unique life was pointing them. In doing so, gratitude became a way of life built into their daily routines, and, more importantly, into their personal character. My Irish hosts prompted me to understand why birthday parties are important expressions of thankfulness for the lives of the people we celebrate and honor. In each case, gratitude is a joyful response to the good fortune of having known those to whom and for whom we are grateful. But each of these examples prompts us to reflect about the obstacles to gratefulness. Jack and Rose endured years of frustration and sadness because of their son's condition and their family's isolation. And most parents encounter waves of frustration in coping with the tantrums of ungrateful children, whether it is at a birthday party that they know is on some level wasteful and even misleading to their children, or a summer vacation that required exhausting effort to arrange, or simply cooking a healthy dinner. And yet teaching gratitude to our children is an inescapable responsibility of parenting that requires perseverance, a great deal of perseverance.

Perseverance is required because the personalities of our children are dominated by a thirst for what they do not have. They always seem to want more: more candy, more toys, more time before bed, more autonomy. Self-centeredness and ingratitude are, undoubtedly, an inevitable part of growing up. How could it be otherwise? From the earliest days, children receive what they need from their parents. It is an asymmetrical relationship: the child needs care and the parent provides it. When he cries, the mother brings food, a clean diaper, or a warm blanket. As they grow we support and defend them, help them with homework, sign them up for soccer, basketball, or music, and drive them to and from each of these events. These provisions come to be expected by the child long before they can care for themselves or even say "thank you."

The more we provide for our children, the more they tend to see themselves as the center of the world. The more we feed them from the outside, however, the greater the risk they will feel empty on the inside. The emptier they feel on the inside, the more they feel they need from the outside. This is one way of understanding why selfishness, which is the primary obstacle to gratitude, takes root in children. But if we think back on our own lives, we are sure to find examples of our own selfishness and ingratitude. Such recollection is not only a useful exercise to quell the frustration that we feel from time to time in response to the selfishness of our children; it can also be a step toward finding our own sense of gratitude by reinterpreting latent memories from our own personal life story.

MEMORY AND MEANING: TRANSFORMING STORIES OF SELFISHNESS

It was late August and summer vacation in the Irish midlands was winding down. My uncle's house, the house where my mother grew up, was directly across the street from a hurling field surrounded by ancient stone walls that doubled as a cow pasture in the evening. The cows casually left brown dung-pies scattered about and, as much as we tried to avoid them, our feet frequently found soft yet unpleasant landings at the end of our child-length strides. Each year the village hosted a sports day at the field. At the end of the day there was a final race for each age group. This was the race that we all wanted to win, and there were prizes given to those who placed first, second, or third. I had more competitiveness than speed as a youngster, and I rarely won foot races. This day was no different, though I did manage to squeak out a third-place finish. I wasn't terribly disappointed with the result and looked forward to the award I would receive at the end of the day. When the award came, however, I became distraught. The third-place award was a small, silver cup while the second place prize was a ball. I wanted the ball, something I could play with, not a "stupid" cup. I took the cup with me across the street to my uncle's house and walked into the sitting room where I put on a display of such childish ingratitude that my memory of it aroused powerful feelings of embarrassment for years after.

My uncle was a quiet but engaging man. He quietly enjoyed having kids swirling around his knees. His demeanor was the perfect antidote to too many screaming voices in one house, as there often was when my family stayed with his for weeks each summer. His tricks and teases made us laugh. As I carried out my tantrum over not getting the award

I wanted, neither he nor my mother reacted as I expected. They were calm, watching and listening without smiling or scolding. They let my antics play themselves out and carried on with their conversation over tea by the low fire my uncle lit to take the chill out of the cool late-summer air.

I was caught off guard by their lack of response and left the room feeling empty, as if I hadn't gotten my money's worth from the tantrum. Not willing to go away completely empty-handed, I carried the "stupid" cup with me to bed and lay awake thinking about what I did. My thoughts moved from not winning the event to not getting the award I wanted to my tantrum. By now my emotions had settled. I could no longer remember what I was so mad about and so began to carefully examine every feature of the simple three-inch cup. I pulled the black plastic stand off and snapped it back on. I held it by its tiny handles protruding like little mouse ears from both sides. I imagined lifting it over my head in a victory celebration. And I thought about bringing it downstairs the next morning to drink orange juice from it.

As I reached for the orange juice at the breakfast table the next morning, my aunt cautioned against using the cup as a drinking vessel because it might stain. Instead, she suggested that I place it on the mantel of the fireplace next to the awards my uncle had won as a hurler. We walked into the sitting room where just twelve hours earlier I was doing my best to show how ungrateful a child could be, and she moved items on the mantel to make room for my cup. She carried a chair across the room for me to stand on. I climbed up and placed the cup on the fireplace. The cup stayed there for the remainder of our time in Ireland, and I proudly showed it to everyone who came into the room. I brought it home at the end of the summer and polished it regularly. Thirty years later, it remains a fixture among my awards, and one for which I am most grateful.

As I engage memories of childhood missteps, I recognize that their meanings change and deepen. Rather than episodes I would prefer to forget, they have become opportunities for understanding decisive events in my life. These memories are branded deeply into consciousness because in childhood there is an unobstructed path to the hidden and formative canyons of the mind. Years later, prompted by who knows what, these memories spontaneously reemerge, often with the emotions that originally accompanied them. For a second or two we smile or cringe in a slight bodily contraction as the scene plays in the private theater of the mind. Pleasant memories we allow to linger, even willing them to stay, though they usually evaporate in front of the will's request. The opposite seems to happen with the bothersome ones. We will them away, but defiantly they finish their scene like the gossiping driver who holds up traffic to finish a conversation. Emotions tend to dictate the length and intensity of these scenes in the memory, and their spontaneity seems to leave little room for a director. And yet when we turn our attention to these memories, their place in our personal narrative often becomes less unsettling and more meaningful.

By reflecting on past experiences and the feelings that accompanied them, it became clear to me that the virtue of gratitude can be slow to develop and blossom. With patience and a willingness to understand the past from a more mature perspective of adulthood, however, we can string together years and decades of our lives in an ever more coherent story. Memory is not just a storehouse of snapshots, a musty archive of isolated episodes from the past: memory is the faculty from which we build our ever-deepening life-narrative. By turning inward to our past and actively trying to understand it from new and broader perspectives of the present, we can make sense of things we did and didn't do, some of which we wish we did and didn't do. We find real meaning in what previously seemed senselessly selfish, in memories we might prefer to forget. It is tempting to ignore or repress unpleasant memories, but to do so is impossible because our past shapes who we are, and what our antics meant when we were children is not what they mean to us today. That is not to dismiss them. In taking the time to understand memories, we can do more than recall childhood tantrums and selfishness: we can shape them into a meaningful personal story.

By looking inward to understand the actions, memories, and feelings of our past, we also shed new light on our relationships with others. By recalling these relationships, we reveal what others have done for us and to us. As children we are unaware of how dependent we are. But as adults, we can look back to understand and transform the selfishness of the screaming child or the inconsiderate schoolboy into gratitude for a loving mother and uncle, and for an aunt who thoughtfully found a place to display my cup. I find this a great source of resolve as I witness my own children move through their bouts with self-centeredness and the inevitable frustrations that grow from it.

Looking to the past is not always easy for parents to do. Most of the things we are concerned about as parents are in the future. Will my daughter make the high school team? Will she be accepted into the right college? Will I be able to afford the tuition? Will she find a job? Will she be happy? Along the way, we teach our children hygiene, manners, and household responsibilities, the skills and know-how to take care of themselves as adults. It is inevitable that we devote most of our attention to what we don't have, to what is not in place, to what we hope for. Most of our concerns, especially as parents, are about the future.

Gratitude, on the other hand, is concerned primarily with the past— to what one already has or has had. As long as we are looking toward the future, to what is not yet and what, by necessity, we cannot yet have, we tend to overlook what there is to be grateful for. Sometimes, if we are fortunate, we are reminded of our forgetfulness and lack of gratitude and our gaze is turned to what is worthy of thankfulness.

TOUGH LESSONS

If it is good fortune to be reminded of what we have, perhaps it is a parent's responsibility to provide our children with reminders from time to time of what they have. When it comes to learning the value of gratitude, we hope they learn from watching and imitating us. Thinking back on our own bouts of childhood selfishness, however, we realize that children face a difficult challenge in cultivating the virtue of gratitude. In giving them what they need, and much of what they want, we set up expectations: they simply ask and, most of the time, receive. These expectations, combined with the innate selfishness of childhood, some-times require us to provide direct lessons.

Barry Snyder provided his son, Peter, with a direct reminder on a re-cent trip to the store. As he placed his goods on the counter to pay, Pe-ter asked for a candy bar. Barry saw nothing wrong with his son having the treat, so he bought it and handed it to him while the cashier packed the bag. His son began to open the wrapper as he turned to leave the store. Barry waited, hoping his son would say "thank you" as they walked out the door. Not hearing it immediately, Barry quickened his pace to get closer to his son. When the boy lifted the bar to take his first bite, Barry swiped it from his hand and told him, "The transaction isn't over until you say thank you." He dumped the candy bar in the next garbage he passed. A tough lesson, to be sure; but one well taken.

Several years later, Peter was the last player on his team to receive his trophy at the year-end basketball award ceremony. I had heard from other parents that Peter had never played on the team. He showed up at every practice and every game only to end up sitting on the bench. When I heard this, I assumed that the team was competitive and intent on winning. Then I discovered that they had won only two games in the least competitive division. One would think that Peter might get frustrated, if not angry, in such a situation. Many adolescents would give up; Peter did not. And when the coach introduced him to receive his award, we learned something unique about Peter. After every game and every practice, not only did Peter not get angry or sulk: he made a point of saying, "Thank you, Coach," before leaving the gym.

POLITENESS ON THE WAY TO GRATITUDE

When we remind our children to say "please" and "thank you," we are sowing the seeds of gratitude, which we hope will blossom at some later time, coming from inside of themselves, not as a response to a parent's directive. When gratitude grows into a virtue, it becomes a part of one's character, not something we simply do or express periodically. The journey to gratitude that begins with childish self-centeredness and passes through politeness on the way to virtue can take decades. Patience and persistence is required on the part of parents as they continue to insist that their children say "thank you."

We teach our children politeness as we recognize that it is not the final end in the development of a virtuous character, and that it is in fact very fickle. Politeness needs support from other virtues. Yet virtue does start with politeness. We want them to learn manners as they learn to speak, before they know the difference between right and wrong. We want politeness to be a part of their natural responses to the world, so that it is effortless when appropriate. In telling them to say "please" and "thank you," we are teaching them to look outside of themselves to recognize and acknowledge the help and the good will that they receive and depend on from others.

HUMILITY VERSUS SELF-CONTENTMENT

To be grateful for what we have, however, is not the same as resting content with what we have. There is a critical difference between those who think they "have it made" and see no need to work at improving themselves, and those who see the world through the lens of gratitude. The grateful understand that they are the beneficiary of a gift or act of kindness that is beyond what was earned. This recognition is accompanied with a sense of humility and a desire to do better, do more, if only for the one who bestowed the original favor. In contrast, the parent who thinks he's "made it" says, "If it was good enough for me, it's good enough for my kids." In some cases this is true, but it is not an excuse for failing to work to improve things. Improvement can be achieved in many ways. For some, it is a matter of lifting a family out of financial hardship; for others, it is overcoming illness. Ultimately, however, our achievements are for naught if they do not foster an improvement of character.

One of the greatest gifts parents can give to the next generation is the opportunity to become better people, to be more virtuous than themselves. This may involve improving the financial circumstances of a family or raising the educational standards, but it doesn't stop there. It involves finding enduring principles to live by such as truth, justice, self-reliance, and compassion, all of which are the offspring of gratitude.

THE GRATITUDE PARENTS ALREADY HAVE

There are many obstacles parents must overcome to be moved by grace and gratitude. The uncertainties of the future seem to hold our attention like a magnet. Those who can resist this pull in order to look inward and backward, to what they already have and can be grateful for, are better able to address their doubts and challenges with balance and inner strength. Once we start down a considered path of grace, a path on which we learn to be grateful, we realize just how much there is to be grateful for. Beneath the frustration, anxiety, and confusion that can dominate a parent's life, there is the enduring gift of life that animates ourselves and everything we see: this is the ultimate gift and the fundamental source of gratitude.

As parents, we interact with the animating source of life most immediately by watching and nurturing the growth and development of our children. If we allow ourselves, we can find a deep sense of gratitude through them. And while we struggle to instill a sense of gratitude in our children, it is, ultimately, we who benefit most from the virtue and the strength of gratitude. It is our privilege to acknowledge that all of the care, all of the lessons, and all of the resources we devote to the well-being of our children are a sign that we are already grateful for them. Joy comes with the recognition that this work is gratitude itself. In gratitude, our loving response to the gift of a child—our life's work—becomes life's greatest joy.

While gratitude is almost a lost virtue in today's world of anxiety, excess, and greed, it is usually not as far away as it seems. The turning point that allows us to find it can be subtle and difficult to locate, like a narrow turn hidden between the high ditches of a dark country road. This turn remains hidden to us most of the time because it leads inward and backward when we are accustomed to looking outward and moving forward. It is a temporary turn away from the future of what is not yet, not real, of expectations yet to be fulfilled and toward an awareness of what is and what has been, what is real and cannot be denied or taken away. The past has more to offer than the future when it comes to gratitude since we can be grateful only for what we already have or have had. If we learn how to look for it, we will find that it waits quietly beneath the turbulent surface of headstrong household battles. Unlike the child who can't easily get out of his selfish tirade, parents can adjust their view to see things unfold in a different light. When we do, we can uncover the virtue of gratitude, a source of strength and the basis of a joyful disposition that wants to share itself. The joy of gratitude makes it worth searching for, especially when chore after parenting chore seems so thankless.

The Buddhist monk and teacher Tich Naht Hahn astutely points out that a child can never adequately repay his parents for all that they do. The best we can do, he advises, is to be happy in their presence. In the end, happiness is what parents want for their children. To see it come to fruition is their greatest reward and the best sign of gratitude on the part of a child. But the reverse is also true. What a child wants most from parents is to see them happy. This is the most effective way a parent can show gratitude to and for their children. Sometimes we need to delve into our own past to reconstruct the stories and times that we lacked gratitude. In doing so, we might learn that what we were looking for in episodes of selfishness as a child no longer eludes us. Then we can begin to be grateful for what we are, what we were, what we have and what we don't have. This is what we want to show our children because their presence is what we are most grateful for. And it is precisely the gift of their life that makes us understand and enjoy the gift of our own lives.

6

FORGIVENESS

After the year-end gathering of the local dart club, I traveled with my weekend hosts to a pub on a dark, almost indecipherable country road outside Dungannon in County Tyrone, Northern Ireland. We walked around the back of a small, one-story farmhouse and entered a windowless door that had several heavy bolts holding it firmly shut. In their unmistakable Northern accents, my companions let those inside know that I was a friend. The door opened and closed quickly and, with a slight arm gesture toward a makeshift counter, three pints were pouring before we sat down.

The damp room hadn't been painted in a long time, and hollows were worn into the vinyl-tile floor. The seats were hard, square-shaped benches surrounding wobbling folding tables. Over time, measured by the descent of stout in our pint-glasses, voices grew more animated. There was the occasional joke and laugh, but there was a palpable undercurrent of tension that would not allow humor to take root.

I occasionally took a break from the effort required to understand the sharpness of the accents to peer around the room. Looking past faces, I spotted small round holes randomly scattered on the walls. Waiting for an opportunity, I asked one of the men I came with about the holes. Leaning over to my left, I posed the question so that only he could hear, expecting him to reciprocate with an equally quiet response. Instead, my question was like fuel on a simmering fire. My companion sat up straight, his face hardening into a fixed seriousness, and spoke louder than everyone, without yelling, "Hy, lads, Seamus here wants to know what the holes in the wall're. Do any'ye want to tell'em or will I?"

Floodgates opened and waves of emotion poured out, transporting me in an instant to a different world. "You can see those holes because we spent hours cleaning me brother's blood off the walls last week after the dirty British bastards shot him," one of them began. "They'll not get away with this one," another added. "Ther'll be no peace until those fuckers are dead or gone. We're tired of listening to people talk about peaceful solutions when our families are being murdered." Mumblings of agreement spread around the room.

Never before, nor since, have I felt such emotion, such anger, or such desire for revenge. I had stumbled into a freshly wounded tribe, their pulsating emotions of grief raw and exposed. The intensity of their words, like a quick-rising tide, lasted for another pint and suddenly receded, though I know it wasn't gone. The makeshift bar was disassembled, kegs hidden, lights quenched, and the doors locked. As we walked toward the car, I was handed the keys and told to drive. "If we're stopped, we might have some chance with a Yank driving." I sobered up immediately and concentrated intently on navigating each night-blackened turn.

The next morning, I dressed for the wedding I was in the North of Ireland to attend and entered the small kitchen where several members of the groom's family were gathered. I was guided to a chair at the end of the table and a full breakfast. When I finished, the groom's brother, my escort to the dart club the night before, poured a clear, pungent glass of *poiteen* and without saying a word walked away to put on his coat. Disguising great effort, I tried to take the drink as casually as it was presented. I secretly stiffened my palate into a rigid funnel and somehow managed to get the liquid inside me.

Just beyond the front door, three cars stood, motionless, in a line. The groom's parents got into the first, the groom and three others into the second, and some of his brothers and sisters into the third. I was standing next to two small children and their mother outside the front door. Since we were the only ones not yet in a car, I figured that this was the family I would be traveling with. The cars idled for a few minutes until a thin, red-headed man emerged from the side of the house. He walked deliberately as far as the groom's car, stood upright, and pointed a rifle into the air firing three loud shots. The cars began to drive slowly through the yard-gate. As we got into his car, the children were crying hysterically.

I wanted to comfort the children as I rode in the back seat with them, but I was afraid to give the driver less than my undivided attention, as he offered an impassioned speech about the injustices of British rule in Northern Ireland. His primary concern was the economic disparities and the lack of employment for Catholics. His anger was palpable as he spoke over the cries of his children, still frightened by his gunshots. He didn't mention the shooting that recently took place in the makeshift pub I had visited the night before, but it was clearly on his mind.

Although his words were fueled with rage as we drove to the wedding, his rhetoric was compelling, mainly because it somehow wasn't clouded by his passion: it was measured and factual. He quoted detailed statistics to support the charge that his community was being decimated by economic injustice. Men were losing jobs or couldn't find any because they were Catholic. Those who had jobs faced other roadblocks such as denied applications for permits to build houses. These injustices cut at the dignity of the Catholic community, and no man would stand for it, he declared.

All the men and women I encountered that weekend showed the same oddly compelling combination of anger and focus. They did not intend to succumb to what they perceived as unjust oppression, but it weighed on them. Whether in the car, the house, or the pub, resentment and calculation filled the space. In the midst of their anger, there was resolve and detailed figuring on how they would respond or resist.

There seemed to be no place for forgiveness. The crying children in the back seat of the car, listening to their father's angry description of the injustice and indignity he faced, indicated little hope for forgiveness to emerge in the next generation. As we rolled past the hedgerows, I wondered if cycles of hatred, vengeance, and repercussion would outlast us all. Wounds of every sort were deep, and the problems that caused them were ongoing. With nobody acknowledging fault for lives ruined though murder and exploitation, and no prospects of change on the horizon, forgiveness seemed impossible. They could consider forgiveness only after the sources of their suffering were addressed and those who committed crimes against them acknowledged their wrongdoing. Otherwise, forgiveness, to them, was merely a form of surrender.

This is a prevalent view of forgiveness inasmuch as it is grounded in the reality of human emotions. When we experience strong emotions, especially negative ones caused by the transgressions of others, it takes great effort to wrestle free from them. It seems to be a natural human response to respond in kind—"an eye for an eye." Parents understand the emotions that lead to such responses. We've all seen children push parents into the throes of heated frustration seemingly every bit as intense as the frustration of the father who drove me to the wedding in Northern Ireland. And just as he put the pursuit of justice before the possibility of forgiveness, parents, too, act to restore equilibrium in the home by squashing or punishing the transgressions of children. They are grounded for breaking curfew, denied TV for missing homework, and chores are added for being dishonest. These punishments are often levied in the heat of anger and discussed later, when emotions have subsided. When parents are pushed to the limits of tolerance, their response is often aligned with the passion and frustration of my Northern Irish hosts. Forgiveness is conditional and withheld until the conditions have been met.

Of course, the conditional approach to forgiveness is not unique to my Irish hosts or to parents who impose conditions on their children before they offer forgiveness. We have seen relatives of victims of the attacks that took place in New York and Washington in 2001 wrestle with deep-seated emotions arising from their loss. As with my Northern Irish hosts, their ability to forgive is compromised by the absence of remorse in those responsible for the murders. There are other reasons people withhold forgiveness. In *The Sunflower*, Simon Wiesenthal shares his experience of being pulled off a work-line in a concentration camp to visit a dying Nazi soldier.[1] The soldier requested to speak with a Jew to ask forgiveness for atrocities he had committed against the Jewish people. He confessed his crimes to Wiesenthal, and asked to be forgiven. Wiesenthal offered only silence. Even if he was inclined to forgive the dying man, he couldn't, he thought, because no individual has the authority to forgive simply on the basis of being a member of a victimized race. Only the victims themselves can forgive their perpetrators and one cannot forgive on behalf of one who is dead.

On the other end of the forgiveness spectrum are the Amish of Lancaster, Pennsylvania, who suffered the horrific massacre of their children in October 2006. Their response to the tragedy astonished the world when they offered forgiveness to the perpetrator, Charles Roberts, who killed himself in the carnage. They visited his wife and parents, prayed with them, and even set up a fund to help her with expenses. While this extraordinary act of forgiveness is all but incomprehensible to most of us, Kraybill and colleagues explain in *Amish Grace* that the Amish did not just suddenly decide that they would forgive Charles Roberts or offer their sympathy and understanding to his family.[2]

Forgiveness has been a part of the Amish culture for hundreds of years and is reinforced every day in their prayers and actions. The line in the Lord's Prayer that says "Forgive us our trespasses as we forgive those who trespass against us" is a centerpiece of their culture, of their daily routines, and, hence, of their understanding about forgiveness. As people of faith, salvation is their ultimate goal and this will only be achieved if they forgive others in the way that God forgives them. Their ability to forgive is strengthened by their worldview in which they enjoy a relationship with a personal God who, they believe, forgives them for their failings: God's forgiveness comes most readily to those who offer forgiveness to others.

To some, the religious motivation for forgiving is dangerous because it postpones one's well-being now for a reward later. In doing so, this line of thinking goes, there is little room for adequate grieving and healing. Like a surgical wound that must heal from the inside out, deep emotional wounds take time. If denied this time, wounds can become infected. Emotionally, this means one succumbs to bitterness, resentment, or even despair. So while the Amish response to devastating tragedy shows just how far human beings can go to forgive and avoid being overcome with the despair of negative emotions, we look to their example with caution. Forgiveness forgoes retaliation and revenge as well as the protracted negativity they produce, but when offered too quickly it also risks the danger of inadequately mourning one's loss or hurt.

These are tensions with which parents regularly struggle in order to find a healthy balance toward forgiveness. Most parents find themselves fluctuating between the responses of the Irish and Amish, between conditional and radical forgiveness. We get angry at our children for their transgressions and want them to learn from their mistakes. This is why we sometimes impose punishments. But we also want to restore a loving relationship as soon as possible, and this requires letting go of our disappointments and demands. As parents, we are faced with the task of balancing these competing emotions within family relationships that might already be filled with tension. The capacity to forgive at the appropriate time and in the appropriate way is a gift to family life. It can break cycles of contempt that corrode family relationships and serve as a powerful turning point toward restoring these relationships. And while offenses within families are rarely as traumatic as those portrayed in this chapter, lingering grudges often do build up over time until we find ourselves deeply resenting someone we also love.

TO FORGIVE A CHILD

According to contemporary French philosopher Andre Compte-Spoonville,[3] there isn't much to think about when it comes to parents forgiving their children. Parents do not forgive their children, he suggests, not because they won't, but because they don't have to. A parent's unconditional love for her children supersedes the need for forgiveness. Unconditional love "can rise above any possible misdeed, any possible offense," Compte-Spoonville writes.[4] Unconditional love enables the parent to accept the child back, even after grave offenses.

A parent can accept a child back, however, only because the relationship with the parent has been broken or wounded. Every wound must heal, and the way a wound heals has a lasting effect on both one's health and the health of a relationship throughout life. Deep wounds require delicate care. Forgiveness is like the balm that is applied to a flesh-wound to keep it clean and clear of infection, allowing it to heal more efficiently. Even relationships grounded in love do not escape wounds. In fact, those who love the most often suffer the deepest wounds.

In earlier chapters, we've encountered parents who were disappointed or wounded by their children. Emily Bookman's study habits and lack of interest drove her father, Will, to act out in ways that made

him feel guilty. In order to overcome his guilt and repair their relationship, he had to reassess his expectations of Emily. This involved
learning to accept her as she was and then work from there. Sean
Healy endured the embarrassment of his son mocking him outside a
neighborhood bar and his own inept, violent response when he tried to
bring the teenager home. He soon discovered his son was an alcoholic.
After the shock and disappointment wore off, he also realized that he
had to accept his son as he was if he was going to be of any help to him
moving forward. The acceptance of where a child is, faults and all, is
the first stage of forgiveness.

Accepting someone where he is in his life, however, is not the same
as accepting or condoning individual actions or misdeeds. It is the work
of the parent to teach and guide children away from mistakes, and to
resist them when they are defiantly and dangerously moving toward
them. Parents regularly navigate the tension between teaching, enforcing rules, punishing—in other words, not fully accepting where they are,
and accepting them and their mistakes without recrimination. This side
of the tension—acceptance—is often more difficult to embrace, but it
is important that we do in fact accept children where and how they are
if we are to see the issues that need to be addressed. Without accepting
the child where she is, the second stage—the gift—cannot be given. The
gift of forgiveness, which is the gift of freedom, liberates an offender
from his offense. It is the gift of understanding that eliminates grudges.
It is the gift of looking forward together, in support, rather than looking
down in judgment. It is the gift of demonstrating that joy, commitment,
passion, and fun can be achieved in ways that are not self-destructive,
as they are to the teenager who abuses alcohol. When the anger and
hurt resulting from a child's offense subside, the parent recognizes that
the child is in chains. We sometimes say, "If they knew better, if they
knew the suffering they would endure as a result of their miscues, they
surely wouldn't choose them." But in our clearer moments we recognize
that mistakes are an integral part of a child's development: they often
do choose the wrong path, even when they know better. What more
evidence do we need that they are in chains?

Having endured the consequences of similar mistakes in our own
lives, parents have the advantage of (fore)seeing alternatives. We wish
we could protect children from their mistakes and the suffering that

accompanies them, and we work hard to do so. But when we cannot, we forgive them by understanding their predicament. This can be very difficult, especially when their mistakes cut to the heart of what we perceive to be our jobs as parents. Although the murderous, tragic circumstances of the Irish and Amish examples plumb the deepest waters of human emotion, considering them can be instructive even when we need to navigate the more shallow pools of our parenting.

A FATHER'S DISAPPOINTMENT

I recently spoke with a colleague who was bothered by an unusual absence of phone calls from his father. Although Bill was almost thirty, married, and living only a few miles from his father's house, he regularly received a few phone calls a week, usually in the evening when he got home from work. When the phone calls stopped for a week or so, he surmised that there was something wrong. He thought back on the previous few weeks to see if he could identify a cause for the silence. He wondered if he had done something to offend his father. After some thought, he zeroed in on a party he recently attended for a neighborhood friend. He met several old friends at the party, including some he knew through his parents. One of those friends was an old-timer named Terry, who was known as a prolific gossip. When Bill took a break from the party to step outside for a cigarette, he met Terry doing the same. They shared a light and did some catching up.

Terry lived up to his reputation and the next day called Bill's father to share the news of their chance encounter, including the details of sharing a cigarette. Although Bill had been smoking for many years, he hid it from his parents, who openly expressed revulsion at the practice whenever they saw it. Bill knew it was a silly habit and a powerful addiction. Like many smokers, he started in order to defy his authoritarian father, without anticipating the strength of its addictive claws. In response to the rational thought that he should quit, a voice in his mind always countered that smoking is a free choice that nobody should interfere with. In his better moments, he knew this was a poor rationalization for his habit, though it was usually enough to weaken his resolve to resist.

Bill's father was angry about the news for a few reasons. First, he hated hearing negative stories about his son from a gossip. He imagined the gossiping friend's glee coming at his expense. Second, it hurt him to hear that his son was engaging in such a self-destructive activity. He could never understand smoking, and hearing that his son was doing it infuriated him. Third, it was as if one of the most basic lessons in life that he hoped to impart to his son was being ignored. He interpreted smoking as both stupid, a characteristic no parent wants to attribute to his son, and defiant, a clear rejection not only of his paternal influence, but also of what Bill's father held to be sensible.

A reflective man by nature, Bill's father usually turns inward to contemplate and brood when things don't go his way. On this occasion, the turn inward led him to consider what he had accomplished in his seventy-plus years of life. The darkness of his mood made him question his success at what was most important to him—the dignity and well-being of his children. His silence toward his son was a response to the disappointment he felt upon learning of Bill's inability or unwillingness to meet basic expectations he held for Bill. He never thought his expectations were too high. He knew that he was difficult to get along with from time to time but, on the whole, he thought of himself as both a good man and a good father. He provided everything his children needed, he thought, far beyond the basics that included college and graduate school tuition, subsidized rent, and a continuously open door to his own house. As he recounted the many things he had done and the sacrifices he had made as a parent, the thought of Bill smoking with an old geezer he didn't particularly care for angered him.

In silence, he wrestled to come to terms with Bill's defiance, his own embarrassment, his lack of influence, and his need, finally, to repair their relationship. Although he could never bring himself to accept his son's habit, he knew, surely, that he would have to accept his son nonetheless. He began by acknowledging that he no longer had direct influence over his son and that, as a young adult, his son would have to find his own way out of the self-destructive habit. Recognizing this fact gave Bill's father some breathing room. It relieved him of the burdensome feeling that somehow he had to fix the problem. Once he acknowledged to himself that he couldn't fix his son's problem, he was able to remind

himself that his son is more than his habit. And while he disdains smoking, the best and, perhaps, only way he might help—he thought—was
to accentuate those dimensions of his son's life and of their relationship
that were in fact very strong.

He allowed himself the temporary comfort of favorably comparing
Bill's accomplishments with those of his friends' sons. At least his son
didn't fail out of a prestigious college while selling drugs, as the oldest
son of his closest friend did. That episode cost Tim Madigan tens of
thousands of dollars in tuition and legal fees along with the embarrassment of national media scrutiny. He also reminded himself that Tim
Madigan forgave his son and provided enormous assistance to him as
he built a business and a house for his young family. Nor did Bill steal
money from his father's bank account to pay gambling debts, as Paddy
Murphy's son did a few years back. Paddy never forgave his son, and
they haven't spoken since. And Bill certainly didn't harm anyone else, as
Mickey Moran's son did when he killed three companions in a car wreck
as he drove home drunk from a party.

By recalling these examples, Bill's father discovered a perspective
that enabled him to separate the habit from the person. In the space of
this separation, the seeds of forgiveness took root. These comparisons
demonstrated that Bill's smoking habit need not be interpreted as such
a grave offense. Left untreated, however, the feelings that surround an
annoying habit like smoking can drive a wedge between family members
and destroy relationships. In fact, it is the habits of our daily lives that
sometimes offend the most, especially those with whom we are closest.
As angry as Bill's father was, he wanted to prevent bad feelings from
becoming entrenched.

As this simple story shows, it is in the confines of daily household trials and tensions that we are tossed between the desire for restitution,
as the Irish were in the previous example, and the extraordinary ability
to forgive the worst offenses, as the Amish did in response to the attack
on their children. On the one hand, we want to play a positive role in
shaping sound habits in our children. We do this by encouraging their
strengths, correcting mistakes, and punishing offenses. When children
are out of line, consequences help them to learn. Analogous to the Irish
pursuit of justice before forgiveness, a parent's punishment of a child is
sometimes necessary in the formation of sound habits for living.

On the other hand, unconditional forgiveness can be an essential element in preventing unnecessary corrosion in the relationship between parents and children. The Amish show us how powerful and far-reaching forgiveness can be as they remind us of the biblical passage from the gospel of Matthew 18:21–23:

> Then Peter came to Jesus and asked, "Lord, how many times shall I forgive my brother when he sins against me? Up to seven times?" Jesus answered, "I tell you, not seven times, but seventy times seven times."[5]

For the Christian, there are no limits to how many times we should forgive. Jesus reinforces this point in the parable of the prodigal son. It is the wayward son for whom the father throws the greatest feast, regardless of how long he has been away or what he has done. This parable seems to reverse the direction of faith. Ordinarily we speak of the gift or the challenge of human faith in God, but this passage implies an inexhaustible faith in human beings: a faith that no matter how far one has strayed, a person is always worth being welcomed home. In this way, forgiveness is one of the greatest gifts a parent can offer to a child, though certainly not the easiest. This is an unconditional faith that is offered even before the parent hears the story of where his son has been, before the smoking stops. This gift requires a parent to dig deep into the core of his being where the wellspring of love resides, allowing that spring to rise and push aside grievances and grudges that come with a child's offenses and miscues.

And we need to remind ourselves that the gift of forgiveness offered to a child is also a gift to the one who forgives. It is a gift that not only gives the child a fresh start in the eyes of a parent, but also frees the parent to love her child again. This is a powerful gift parents can give to their children and themselves. But it is also a gift that can be offered by children to their parents, which is good news for parents, who can be every bit as flawed as their children.

ASKING FOR FORGIVENESS

The choice to forgive not only liberates an offender from his offense or a victim from the lingering effects of an offense; it also has the ability to release us from our own internal states of oppression. That is, we can oppress ourselves, weigh ourselves down with guilt, after we have committed an inappropriate action. As parents, this is vitally important since we are often walking a fence between disciplining a child and offending her, between praising one sibling and neglecting another. While we strive for balance, sensitivity, and fairness, we often miss. And even when we are being fair, children can see it otherwise. It is often difficult for us to see the ways we hurt children as we go about our adult lives. In failing to notice our offenses, we run the risk of alienating our children. In *The Picture of Dorian Gray,* Oscar Wilde captures the way children often view their parents in response to this tendency when he writes, "Children begin by loving their parents; as they grow up they judge them; sometimes they forgive them."[6] Children who can forgive their parents are very fortunate—they are freer to live their lives than those who cannot. Parents add to their children's good fortune when they recognize the need to be forgiven, and ask for it. Too often, we fail to see the need to be forgiven by our children as we meet success after success in other areas of our lives. And yet forgiveness can be a powerfully redemptive act within a family.

We see the redemptive power of forgiveness in *The Death of Ivan Ilych,* Leo Tolstoy's gut-wrenching portrayal of a man who struggles to find an explanation for his suffering in the face of his imminent death.[7] On the surface, Ivan had a good life. In fact, if offered his resume, most people would accept without much hesitation. Ivan was a successful lawyer and judge; he had an upper-middle-class income and a house to match; he had a wife and two children as well as plenty of friends with whom he would spend time. But he was not very good at dealing with the difficulties of life. When his wife became irritable during pregnancy, he worked longer hours. When people needed advice or counsel in his courtroom, he offered only empty and useless courtroom jargon. When he was passed over for promotion, he resented his coworkers and friends, and left his job.

But then Ivan got sick and the table turned. Now he called out for individualized attention, sincerity, and compassion. But almost everyone in his life—his wife, his doctors, his daughter—treated him the way he had treated others. He sought pity; he wanted to be understood; he wanted his questions answered by doctors. Instead, he received only false assurances, official lines, and standard protocols. The deception drove Ivan into despair.

Ivan tried to hold onto his identity and so justify his life. But the more he examined how he had lived, the less there was to defend. As death approached, he felt completely alone, and his search for answers came up empty. After exhausting all possible targets of blame for his misery—his wife, his friends, and God—he had to listen to the innermost voice of his soul. This voice asked him what he wanted. Ivan's response was simply, "To live." Not satisfied, his soul pressed, "To live how?" Ivan now finds himself forced to examine his life more closely, and realizes that the only times he was really happy were in childhood. Every pursuit since, beginning with law school, sacrificed his enthusiasms for life for the sake of approval of those who enjoyed some kind of social status. The realization that life was ebbing away from him in direct proportion to his climb in social stature forced him to admit his life was all wrong.

This is a difficult realization to face on one's deathbed. But Ivan doesn't give up on making sense of his life, and so sets his attention to finding a way to correct it. Just hours before he dies, as he struggles on his deathbed, his flailing hand makes contact with his son who is crying at his bedside. Behind his son stands his wife, whom Ivan had come to despise over the course of their marriage; she too is crying. Finally, through this direct encounter with their sadness and suffering, Ivan is enlightened by the insight he was looking for: all the while that he was blaming others for his unhappiness, it was he who was causing those around him to be unhappy. It is he who is the source of their suffering. With this insight and the feeling of compassion he has for them, Ivan decides he must act. He asks for forgiveness as he finally recognizes his own flaws and the effect he has on his family: he wants to release them from the suffering he has caused them. In doing so, he also releases himself from his own misguided life. As Tolstoy presents it, Ivan's suffering and despair fall away all at once, and he is no longer afraid to die.

This story holds an important lesson for all parents. While we work hard and sacrifice for the well-being of our families, we do not do so flawlessly. As we provide, nurture, and support, we also offend and hurt. And while we all need support and acknowledgment for what we do from time to time, we also need to be forgiven for the mistakes we make. Much of what we say and do seems innocent enough to us, and yet children do receive and internalize so much of what we say and do in unpredictable ways. Many times, the ways they receive our messages are hurtful. To be sensitive to this hurt and to ask them for forgiveness when we recognize it is to let them know that we do respect them and their feelings. It also lets them know that we know we are not always right. They, in turn, learn that it is okay not to be perfect: if we can make mistakes, they too can make mistakes. If we can admit our mistakes, they too can admit theirs. If we seek forgiveness, they can too. Children are usually very forgiving to their parents, but to take this for granted is to miss opportunities for significant growth on the part of parent, child, and the relationship between them.

CULTIVATING FORGIVENESS

These stories reveal the complexity of forgiveness as well as its transformative power. Different people see forgiveness, and its appropriate roles, differently. For the Irish it is conditional. For the Amish it is crucial. As parents, we want to avail of its liberating and transformative power as much as possible. Most of us reside somewhere between the limits of the Irish and the Amish, between justice at all cost and forgiveness at all cost. To negotiate this tension, we will find assistance in cultivating the virtue of forgiveness and apply it in the battles of family life.

Spinoza is, perhaps, the most optimistic philosopher with respect to our ability to transform emotions, an ability that is an essential precursor to offering forgiveness. For him, this transformation begins as soon as we attempt to understand our emotions and what precisely caused them. Most often, the attempt to understand emotions, especially negative ones such as resentment, anger, or hate, reveals that the simple act of attributing the cause of an emotion to another person does not provide an adequate understanding of the emotion. The person I hate may have a role to play in the emotion; for example, she lied to me or she betrayed me and I hate her for it. But if I look beneath the surface and try to understand why she lied or betrayed me, I quickly realize that there are many forces at work in her life. These forces led her to make the decision she made, to act as she did. If she felt like she could have told the truth or not betray me, she would have. But she didn't feel like that. She was in chains. Once I can see this, my intense anger or hatred subsides. This is the power that reason possesses to transform our emotional landscape as well as the power to liberate us from the emotions that keep us from doing what is most important to us and being who we most want to be.

Most of the time, it is not too difficult to understand that a young child is not in complete control of his actions. When he breaks a treasured family heirloom because he ignored your instructions not to play ball in the house, you get angry. It is upsetting to lose something irreplaceable because of a child's defiance. And yet we get past the negative emotions associated with such a misstep more easily with younger children than with older children because our expectations are lower. We know they have less control over their actions, and resistance is a part of their development. The older our children get, however, the more we expect from them. If your middle school student fails a test because she didn't study (when she said she did), you get upset and hold her accountable. But in order to correct the problem, anger will be less effective than understanding for both parent and child; hence the need for understanding. By actively trying to understand the problem, the anger subsides, and you are free to help her improve her study habits. You forgive the trespass, and you are free to move on.

Forgiveness achieves freedom. It not only relinquishes the desire for revenge, but it also liberates one from the negative emotions that linger beyond the initial offense. The longer I am angry, the longer my offender has power over me. A parent who can forgive is free to teach and guide more effectively and more joyfully. More difficult than forgiving another, however, is asking for forgiveness. While forgiving another liberates one from the negative emotions of hate and vengeance, to ask for forgiveness liberates one from the façade of perfection. When a parent asks a child for forgiveness, it tears down this façade and allows the parent to be a person, flawed and all. But it also liberates the child from the pressure of living up to the illusory perfection of a parent.

Forgiveness is a challenging virtue inasmuch as it asks us to abandon the fleeting strength that accompanies negative emotions such as anger and hate and replace it with a higher, serene, and enduring strength. It asks the soldier, the prisoner, or the victim to see the chains around his enemy even when that enemy is placing chains around him. Forgiveness demands a higher vision of the world, a perspective that is not restricted by hate, anger, or vengeance. But, contrary to the views of my Northern Irish friends, forgiveness is not the same as surrender. Although forgiveness relinquishes the call for revenge, it surely does not abandon the quest for justice. With forgiveness, however, the pursuit of justice is calmer, the goal clearer.

For parents, forgiveness is a part of daily life. We don't often think about it because we do it over and over again. We offer the gift of understanding because we know that a child's ability to always make good decisions is limited. We are more motivated to find such understanding with children than with strangers because we love them. But there are times when children go too far and injure that love. These times call for great resolve from the parent to offer understanding, to accept them where they are, especially when we want them to be somewhere else. But to guide them to where they need to be, we need to get past the hurt and the anger. We need to forgive.

To forgive is to give a gift. It is to liberate an offender from his offense while at the same time liberating oneself from the lingering spiritual or emotional pain that results from an offense. The liberation that occurs on both sides of a wounded relationship allows that relationship to heal and to begin growing in a healthy direction. Without forgiveness, healing and growth cannot happen. For parents, it is at least as difficult to ask for forgiveness from our children as it is to offer it. Asking for forgiveness presupposes an admission of guilt, a mistake, and this is something we are reluctant to do with children. We feel as if it might undermine our credibility with them and our authority to make and enforce rules. But to be able to admit mistakes and to ask for forgiveness establishes a different type of credibility that goes much deeper than preserving authority or enforcing rules. To admit a mistake and to seek forgiveness from our children at the appropriate time not only opens a unique space for children to grow: it is also an essential part of how parents grow up.

7

FAITH

If there were a mirror that we could somehow hold up to ourselves as we make our way through any of the turning points discussed in this book, we would see that the engine that drives us through each of them is a unique kind of faith, which I describe as philosophical faith. Unlike religious faith, which is focused on our relationship with a mysterious and transcendent God, philosophical faith begins much closer to home. It is an inner strength grounded in an intuitive insight that gives parents who have it the confidence they need to help them effectively navigate the tumultuous waters of contemporary life. This insight is not easily captured in the concepts of reason and not easily articulated, yet often provides the clearest direction to take in life. Philosophical faith requires patience and silence because it must see and hear beyond the complex surface of things. It recognizes that there may not always be immediate results and easy solutions, and provides the endurance necessary to persevere with long-term efforts. To cultivate this faith is difficult because there are innumerable distractions along the way.

Philosophical faith begins with a faith in oneself. Unfortunately, faith in the self is eroding from the lives of parents, and it is having a negative impact on children, families, and communities. This erosion can be difficult to detect because it often occurs behind the veil of highly successful parents who are competent and confident in so many areas of their lives. If we simply look around, we'll find numerous examples from community activities that can be interpreted as a parent's loss of faith in self.

As I point out in *The Faithful Parent*, there are troubling trends emerging in the world surrounding childhood sporting events.[1] Traditionally, childhood sports were thought to provide a number of benefits to children such as exercise, socialization, and competition. Sports encourage children to challenge themselves, to improve at what they are doing, and to learn what it means to win and to lose. Some also learn that sports are not their thing while others become dedicated to their sport and pursue it seriously. Generations of children have gained invaluable insights about themselves, friendship, competition, fairness, and sacrifice as a result of playing sports.

Several years ago, while watching the first few softball games in which my daughter participated, it occurred to me that the purpose of childhood sports was becoming cloudy. I admired the coaches who patiently guided girls to positions on the field and showed them how to hold the bat. Only a few girls, however, were capable of hitting the ball more than a few feet. The rest swung aimlessly, rarely making contact. As the time passed, I noticed that I wasn't the only one who had difficulty staying interested in the game. Two girls who were playing on the infield had congregated at second base with their baseball gloves on one hand and sticks in the other. They were both on one knee making pictures in the dirt. Another pair walked with their backs to the game as they talked, seemingly having forgotten about the game entirely. With increasing frequency, coaches and parents had to remind their daughters to "pay attention" and "get ready to catch the ball." These reminders became less and less effective as the game wore on.

As the scene unfolded, I began to doubt the usefulness of these games. It didn't seem as though the girls were being challenged or that they were even learning anything about the game. They were getting no exercise and the friends they congregated with were most often girls they already knew from school. After the novelty of wearing a uniform wore off, it seemed as though there was little that the girls could find appealing. They could, after all, draw figures in the dirt at home, and they wouldn't have to be interrupted by adults telling them to pay attention.

These doubts simmered for the last half hour of the game until I heard a coach yell, "Last batter." Relieved that the game was ending, I walked toward the bench to get my daughter and bring her to the car. As I got closer to the field, I noticed a new urgency among the girls that wasn't there during any other part of the game. The girls seemed attentive. They were all facing the batter, hands on their knees, and ready to move. The ball was struck and dribbled feebly away from the tee. The parents and coaches yelled, "Run, keep running!" The batter ran around the infield touching all four bases while a few girls in the field chased the ball, not sure what to do with it once it was picked it up. As the batter jumped on home plate, one of the girls in the field stretched her arms straight into the air and yelled, "Donut Time!" This announcement sent the players from both teams sprinting to their respective benches where there was a box of donuts waiting. I thought this was a special occasion, a birthday party perhaps. But after the second and third game, I became alarmed. As softball season rolled into soccer season, I learned that a parent is assigned to bring a snack to all children's soccer games. These snacks can be donuts, but usually they are some kind of chips and a sugar drink.

I found this practice troubling, not because it is so awful to treat children once in a while, but because of the larger trend that the treats signify. Children are turning up to sporting events to receive confusing messages as to why they are there and what the value of participating is. This was even more evident at a recent soccer game when a mother of one of the players, who was excitedly following the game up and down the sideline, made a spontaneous bargain with her daughter to entice her daughter to stay on the field. Her daughter was more interested in something on the sidelines than in the game and, at one point, sprinted off the field as the ball was coming toward the goal she was defending. The mother ran after her, picked her up and placed her back in the position she was playing. As the daughter again looked to the sideline, away from the action, the mother yelled, "If you stay there, I will get you the toy you've been asking for." The daughter immediately stopped ignoring her mother and responded, "You mean the doll?" "Yes," responded her mother. The little girl turned and ran toward the play.

The parents in these stories are well intentioned, but they demonstrate a loss of philosophical faith on a number of levels. The need to supplement a sporting event with donuts or a toy reveals a loss of faith in themselves, in the games as an independent source of enjoyment, and in the ability of children to find enjoyment in the games they play. Moreover, parents show a lack of faith in the ability of children to learn from simply participating even if they do find it enjoyable. Finally, parents in these situations demonstrate a loss of faith in the value of resisting the conventions that have crept into these activities. In order to reverse these trends and some of the negative effects they generate, parents need to recover the philosophical faith that is eroding from our lives.

THE MEASURE OF GENIUS

As parents, we are entrusted to guide our children toward a healthy adult life. We try to teach and demonstrate the skills that are necessary to be successful as workers, friends, parents, and citizens. Almost all great philosophers and religious leaders agree that one must go beyond the conventions of social norms in order to achieve greatness. It is no different for parents. We must go beyond social conventions if we are to nurture and guide children effectively. This may sound simple, but it is difficult to achieve because society throws so many obstacles in our way.

The pressure to acquire material comforts; to consume; to amass financial wealth, power, or status appeals to that part of the self that we rely on and pay attention to most of the time—the ego-self. The ego is formed, affirmed, and threatened by social norms. This part of our identity is shaped from our relationships in the world, in particular the world of family and friends. It is this part of the self that leads us to look around at our neighbor, coworker, or our child's classmates to see how we measure up by comparison. It is the ego, eager to fit in, that convinces us to bring donuts to a child's game, knowing that it is unhealthy and a diversion from the game. Acceptance, honor, and praise are the currency of the ego-self. And while the ego-self is essential in making our way through the world, for executing day-to-day transactions, it does not inspire or achieve any greatness. Greatness lies in putting the ego-self in its place and finding faith in a higher or deeper Self.

Faith in the ideas of a higher Self is the first dimension of philosophical faith. The belief, without any assurances from our usual social crutches, that there is a dimension of the self that goes beyond the concerns of the ego is where philosophical faith begins. This is the part of the self that Emerson calls *Genius*. Genius, for Emerson, is not a function of IQ. It is a matter of belief. He writes, "To *believe* your own thought, to *believe* that what is true for you in your private heart is true for all men,—that is genius."[2]

Emerson makes it clear that the ideas of the higher self serve us better as a measure of well-being than do social conventions when he writes, "Society everywhere is in conspiracy against the manhood of everyone of its members. . . . The virtue in most request is conformity. Self-reliance is its aversion."[3] Emerson has supreme confidence that we have a measure that rises above mere social conformity and acceptance. For parents, finding the measure of our own genius is essential because, more than most, we feel the weight of social mores hoisted upon us by friends, neighbors, schools, and, perhaps most of all, by our own children.

As parents well know, peer pressure does not end with adolescence. Even as adults, this pressure can cause us to seriously doubt our capacity for great ideas. When this doubt takes root, the ego loses its footing and forgets that it is grounded in the higher self. When the ego loses its footing in the higher self, it clings to the arbitrary winds of praise, honor, power, and status for affirmation. These kinds of affirmation are like fast-food, providing only unhealthy nourishment to the ego. Like the drug addict whose days are programmed around finding the next fix, the ego can become dependent on these external sources of affirmation and orient its entire life around receiving them.

When this occurs, the first dimension of philosophical faith is effectively smothered, and the measure of greatness is lost. The measure of genius is replaced by the external measures of social conformity and acceptance. Greatness becomes something for other people to achieve because one loses touch with the source of his own genius. For parents, this translates into signing the children up for the next activity simply because it is what the neighbors are doing. It means bribing a child to pay attention to a soccer game. And over time, it means teaching children to lose touch with the source of their own genius.

In order to avoid allowing our values and directives from collapsing into mere social conformity, we need to rejuvenate philosophical faith. This begins with a belief in the ideas and values of our higher selves,

even when they are out of step with the ideas and values of society. It requires a willingness to be misunderstood and to persevere when the tide
is moving against us. We all have our own genius to guide us, but without faith in this higher self, we will never begin to search for it. Without
faith, we won't do the work that is required to develop one's self, nor
will we have the gumption to demand the difficult work of children that
builds character. With this faith in place, however, parents will find that
their own measure, what they come to expect of themselves and of their
children, is far beyond anything society will expect of them. This is the
beginning of greatness.

FAITH IN THE WORLD

While philosophical faith begins with faith in the self, it quickly moves
to include faith in the world. Just as faith in the self calls for us to move
beyond the ego-self, faith in the world leads us to trust and interact with
the world on levels that are not immediately apparent to everyday per-
ception. Faith in the world is the belief that there is coherence, unity,
or meaning beneath the constant changes that we encounter in the everyday world. This belief has been an integral part of the philosopher's
journey from the beginning. By turning the light of reason on the world,
which appears to us as constant change, philosophers uncover meaning
and fulfillment that is inaccessible to the nonrational mind.

Reason seeks out and articulates order and meaning in an otherwise
chaotic world. The power of reason has tamed nature and led to ameni-
ties and comforts that could not have been imagined just a couple of
generations ago. The allurement of this reason and all that it has led
to is so great, however, that we tend to overlook the fact that it is not
our primary access to the world. Upon close examination, we find that
reason stands on the shoulders of faith to conduct its business. Without
faith that there is a hidden but intelligible order to the world and that it
is worth getting to know this order, reason would not have the direction
or the motivation to achieve the success that it has. The philosopher's
search then, while executed by reason, is fueled by a faith that, beneath
the apparent chaos and flux of everyday life, the world has something
that is knowable and worth knowing. Those who have carried out this

search know that it is painfully difficult. It is a search that can leave one feeling disoriented and isolated as well as a little insecure from time to time.

Most parents are familiar with the feelings of isolation, disorientation, and insecurity. The task of raising children doesn't come with a how-to manual and often feels thankless as we move from one crisis to the next, never quite knowing if we are doing or saying the right thing. The insecurity of not knowing often leads parents to follow the crowd, to do what others do, sign their children up for the popular activities and buy the trendy toys and clothes. From the prerational and insatiable desires of children to the irrational and defiant decisions of teenagers, parents are constantly challenged to find coherence amid persistent and unpredictable change. And like the philosopher who knows that the search for meaning and truth is never complete, but a series of constant revisions, parents quickly realize that whatever coherence we may arrive at today will likely need to be revised tomorrow.

In the face of the constant change we encounter in the world, there is a powerful tendency to search for permanence, security, and comfort. We often wish that we could simply escape from the chaos of it all. We long for a quiet retreat from the tensions and demands placed on us by children, work, and the world in general. We line up for lottery tickets and dream of a life of contentment in which we do not have to prepare food that children won't eat, worry about mortgage payments, or feel the anxiety of an approaching deadline. But such a life is fantasy and self-deception. It diverts our attention and energy from the actual events we are called to deal with in the world. The legendary pre-Socratic philosopher Heraclitus expressed his disapproval of such a life by comparing it to the life of cattle or dogs who, he said, bark at everyone they do not know.[4] In Heraclitus's mind, there is no need to escape from the world if we understand it properly. Rather than turning away from the world, he urges us to turn into it with all its strife to find meaning, to find coherence, to find the *Logos*. This turn into the world rather than away from it is unsettling, initially, because we abandon what is familiar and come face-to-face with the deep and confusing impermanence of things and the uncertainty and unpredictability that goes with it.

Friedrich Nietzsche explains that there is a reward waiting for those of us who do not try to escape the world and all of its difficulties when he writes that the impermanence and apparent chaos of things is "a terrible, paralyzing thought. . . . It takes astonishing strength to transform this reaction into its opposite, into sublimity and the feeling of blessed astonishment."[5]

Sublimity and blessed astonishment are feelings that await the one who has the faith along with the strength and courage to wade in the midst of the difficulties of an ever-changing tide rather than scramble for shore. The instinct to avoid unpleasantness and impermanence and the longing for contentment, security, and predictability often prevent us from finding the deepest meaning and the highest rewards that can be found by inquiring into nature and the impermanent and changing world. Heraclitus's belief that there is a hidden *Logos* to be uncovered and understood led him to become familiar with the divine presence in the world. His steady gaze enabled him to see the divine dwelling amidst the chaos.

Parents have an opportunity to achieve this same recognition in their children. The fullness of life, of divine presence, is one way of understanding what we experience in loving our children unconditionally, when we step back from the intensity of everyday life to appreciate the beauty and mystery each child conveys in the world. Parents empty themselves in loving their children. In doing so, they make room for receiving the fullness of meaning and (divine) presence in the world. Most of us, however, rarely have time for such appreciation. In meeting the demands of everyday life, therefore, we rely on faith that it is there. And that faith motivates us to search for meaning and coherence in the midst of (household) chaos.

It is when we lose faith in ourselves and faith in the world that we end up confused and confusing our children by acting against our better judgment. This lack of direction and conviction leads us to bring donuts to sporting events. We want our children to enjoy the game. We know that getting a new uniform is exciting to children. We know the children like donuts. And we are sure that children feel special to be a part of a team. Unfortunately, we forget to teach the children what they are supposed to be doing as a part of the team. This forgetfulness is a symptom of a loss of faith in the game, in its structure and nuances that can only be revealed and enjoyed by the persistence of its participants.

If parents no longer trust that the process of learning the game step by step will be enough fun for children, they will never make the effort required to discover that fun. And so we give them the trimmings of the game (uniforms and treats) without the substance. We sugarcoat their activities (sometimes literally) so they are sure to get immediate enjoyment from it.

For those who are given the chance to learn the game properly, there is a much deeper enjoyment. Like the musician who must practice repetitively in order to master her music, an athlete must be repetitive to master the movements and skill of a game. Without repetition, there is no mastery, even of the basics. Without mastery, there is no depth. Without depth, enjoyment is shallow. For one who masters the skill of a game or a piece of music, there are subtleties that will forever elude the novice. These subtleties make the game or the music a completely different experience, a different world, for the child who is exposed to the proper skills and techniques. Discovering and working with the deep structure of these activities, of a game, a sport, or a piece of music, along with the movements and skills that are required to play them, will always be decisively more rewarding to children than uniforms and treats.

Some will discover along the way that sport or music or some other activity that they are exposed to is not enjoyable. But that discovery is a valuable lesson for a child to learn. It is an opportunity for a child to make a decision to leave something behind, even if her friends do not. It is an opportunity to let her parents know that she feels different than they do about an activity. That is, it is an opportunity for a child to discover, form, and express other parts of her emerging personality. By working through these activities, she learns more of who she is and who she is not. This lesson is obscured and delayed, if not lost, when we sugarcoat the activities of children and shield them from the challenging processes of learning a skill properly. By making the games about uniforms and donuts, we are teaching them to be consumers rather than actors. We are teaching them pleasures that come from being passive, rather than pleasures that come from being active and creative. And children are going to need all of the support they can get to resist settling for passive pleasures as they mature into teenagers and adults in a society driven by marketing and consumption.

FAITH IN THE CHILD

In order to be an effective parent, philosophical faith in one's self and in the world is necessary, but not sufficient. Parents also need to have faith in their children. Children are worlds unto themselves. In each child we encounter a unique coalescence of nature and society. The genetic and cultural inheritance of each child is the gift of a rich and complex past. Just as the philosopher must look beneath the surface, beneath the flux of everyday life, in order to discern the meaning and intelligibility the world has to offer, parents need to look beyond the surface of a child's life to appreciate and cultivate the vast depth and potential they carry into the world. This appreciation and cultivation requires faith in what we cannot fully comprehend or see in the life of the child.

As with the world itself, there are dimensions of the child's world that remain hidden and mysterious, beyond the conceptual grasp and beyond the direct influence of parents. Just as any inquiry into the aspects of the world at large generates more questions along with more knowledge, the closer we examine and interact with children, the more we understand and the more questions we have. It is this excess of being, the mysterious and elusive dimensions of the child, that leave room for faith. As theologian Paul Tillich points out, "Faith is uncertain in so far as the infinite to which it is related is received by a finite being. The element of uncertainty cannot be removed, it must be accepted."[6]

Faith, for Tillich, is "a state of being ultimately concerned."[7] When something compels us to be ultimately concerned, it also demands our total surrender. In the Old Testament, Abraham, the father of faith, demonstrates the total surrender of genuine religious faith. He put his life and his son's life in God's hands. In religious faith the relationship is between a finite and an infinite being. One places faith in God with the hope of achieving total fulfillment, which is impossible in the realm of the finite. Through religious faith, we retain the hope of transcending our finitude through the assistance of God.

While the scriptures make it clear that religious faith demands total surrender to God, we often find ourselves lured into putting our faith in lesser things. Some look for fulfillment in wealth, or country, or pleasure. There are all too many examples of people who have made the pursuit of wealth the centering act of their lives. They surrender themselves to the pursuit, believing that wealth will one day provide the fulfillment they seek. Others surrender themselves to a political movement or a life of pleasure-seeking, hoping to find their fulfillment there. Of course, we know the outcome of their misplaced faith. After each success there is the inevitable feeling of emptiness, meaninglessness, and sometimes even desperation. For some, these disappointments eventually lead to a change of course. They place their faith in something more substantial, and the centering act of the personality becomes a healthier site of integration for all of their concerns. For some, the desperation provokes a downward spiral as they try to fill the emptiness with more of what causes it.

For all of us, the act of faith is risky. We can never be sure that we are placing our faith in the right things. We surrender ourselves to something in the hope that we are working toward fulfillment, but we do not know. Whether it is money or God, the end result is beyond our comprehension. So we dive in and commit ourselves to pursuing something of which we see only shadows, the trace of something that is always around the corner or over the next hill. In order to have faith, therefore, one must also have courage. One must persevere in the pursuit knowing that the end result may end up in failure and disappointment. There is, perhaps, no greater risk than the risk one takes in placing his faith in something, because the result of misplaced faith is a loss of meaning in one's life. One discovers that he has surrendered himself to something that is not worthwhile. In choosing our ultimate concern, we are taking on the ultimate risk, which requires the ultimate courage.

But what about a parent's faith in her child? For many parents, children are their ultimate concern. Parents and families orient their lives around the needs and concerns of children. Days are spent at doctor's offices, supervising homework, and shuffling children from soccer to dance to music. Attending to the needs and activities of children requires parents to sacrifice the pursuit of their own interests. They surrender themselves to the well-being of their children. In the process, parents often seek fulfillment, consciously or unconsciously, through their children. The well-being of their children directly affects their own satisfaction and they see the success of their children as a direct reflection of their own success. While the dedication of parents to their children meets the definition of faith as their "ultimate concern," it leaves open the question of whether it is misplaced, misguided, or idolatrous faith.

There is a double risk for parents when it comes to placing philosophical faith in their children. On the one hand, they are placing their faith in what cannot be known, controlled, or comprehended. If Levinas is correct in describing the face of the human other as the trace of the infinite, the child is a parent's most direct and profound access to the infinite. But as the trace of the infinite, the face simultaneously reveals and conceals. It gives us something to know in what it reveals to us. But the more we get to know what is revealed, the more we come to see the mystery hidden in the infinite from which it comes.

Insofar as children are both finite and a trace of the infinite, parents can and indeed must have faith in the infinite and mostly hidden dimension of a child's life. This is the dimension out of which the unique character, resiliency, and mettle of the child will be forged with the assistance of a parent's love, skill, and insight. In the hidden depths of the child's developing personality is the power to become that which we cannot fully anticipate. So parents are faced with the task of simultaneously nurturing and cultivating the seen and unseen dimensions of a child's personality. And these different dimensions are not clearly demarcated. They are interwoven with each other, the one affecting the other in multiple ways. As parents, we are called to focus on the visible, on what we can know, with full awareness that what we deal with in the visible realm affects, and is affected by, the background that we do not know and cannot see.

TOLERANCE, HOSPITALITY, AND FORGIVENESS

The incomprehensibility of the hidden dimensions of a child's life can be exasperating for parents. Often the most difficult situations for parents are those in which there is uncertainty and ambiguity. A child begins to whine, complain, and cry, sometimes for days at a time it seems, and for no obvious reason. The parent tries to soothe her, to understand what is bothering her, but sometimes there is no reasonable answer. The causes of her agitation are unclear to mother and child, making the situation difficult to address. As adolescents, children challenge parents with a full range of mysterious and incomprehensible behavior from brooding in silence to promiscuous sexual relations.

Faced with the difficulties and unpredictability of our children's emerging personalities, it sometimes seems as though even bad news is better than not knowing because it gives us a sense of direction, a point of reference from which we can formulate a strategy and orient our lives. As we saw in the first chapter with Jim Healy and his son, who was silently battling alcoholism, it can be paralyzing when the hidden dimension of a child's life is ambiguous and beyond our comprehension. A parent who is unable to decide, to act, to guide, to nurture, to discipline may begin to feel like a failure. Entrusted with the responsibility to do all of these things, and do them properly, parents are expected to have the appropriate information and strategies. It is as if children, and society at large, are giving parents the message that a sports apparel company uses in one of its advertisements, "Impossible is nothing."

To think the impossible is nothing can be a motivational trick to encourage athletes to push their training beyond the ordinary. But the later writings of French philosopher Jacques Derrida inspire by taking the opposite approach. For him, the impossible is something. In fact, according to Derrida, we need the impossible. We work toward the impossible; we desire it, seek it, and chase it. But unlike the athlete who is seeking to conquer it, the philosopher is more realistic. He knows we can't catch it. It is the very nature of the impossible to remain beyond our grasp. But even in its irreducible elusiveness and otherness, the impossible has a profound effect on us.

For Derrida, working toward the impossible means working for justice, for forgiveness, for hospitality, with the full awareness that the realization of these ideals will be perpetually deferred. These impossible ideals, ironically, make human life bearable. They open the possibility of pursuing those ever-elusive goals that provide the deepest meaning to our lives. If all we ever aspired to could be achieved, the meaning of our lives would be swallowed up by the world of the familiar, the world of our own making, the world of what is all too possible. Our world doesn't allow for pure justice to reign, but without the ideal, injustice becomes acceptable. The abuse and murder of a child is impossible to forgive, but we entertain the hope for the impossible lest our spirit become permanently vengeful.

For Derrida, philosophical faith is a faith in the impossible. It is an affirmation of that which we will never fully own, grasp, control, or even understand. It is a hope for what it is to come, even if it never arrives. For parents, it is the perpetual hope that our children will be happy and fulfilled, knowing that these human conditions are elusive, never complete, and require persistent effort and extraordinary insight. And beyond hope, a parent's faith in the child demands the repeated affirmations of her children along the way, even when they discourage and disappoint. This faith is the affirmation of what we don't see, of what they don't display, but what we long for and wish for them. It is demonstrated repeatedly in a parent's effort to teach what is valuable and to discipline what is unacceptable, even when we are exhausted, because we have faith that our children can learn principles and parameters that will be useful to their pursuit of a fulfilling life. It is this affirmation and this hope that pushes and enables the parent to see beyond what is apparent, reasonable, familiar, believable, or even possible.

So a parent is called to look beyond the visible for what is not visible while simultaneously focusing on what is in front of her. The hurt bodies and feelings, the tears and tantrums need immediate care while the hidden forces of the child's behavior beckon for our attention, calling like a faint whistle in the shadows, "Hey, Mom, over here." But they're gone before she can look.

Parallel to the task of keeping the visible and the invisible dimensions of a child's developing personality in focus is the task of being simultaneously tolerant, which means placing conditions on our hospitality and also providing unconditional hospitality. As conditional hospitality, tolerance is the attitude that says that you are welcome in my home as long as you abide by my customs and rules. Tolerance makes clear, and retains, the sovereignty of the stronger. Since parents set the customs and rules of the home, it is the parent who decides when to extend tolerance to the child.

At the same time, however, the child calls for the unconditional welcome of hospitality. The hospitality we offer to our children is born out of our primal love for them. Beneath the rules that determine what will and will not be tolerated in the daily lives of any given home, we strive to offer a loving acceptance of the child, even when the incomprehensible dimensions of her personality lead to disappointment, frustration, and anger. This hospitality provides the strength to continue teaching, guiding, caring, and advising, even when it seems like there is nobody listening. Unconditional hospitality rests on the faith that we are moving in the right direction even though we cannot see where we are going or where we are leading our children. It is this faith that provides the parent of a sick child with the motivation to continue searching for the best treatment when information and expertise are scarce. It is the faith that, beneath a child's rebelliousness and defiance, he is somehow absorbing lessons and habits for living that will emerge later and serve him well when he matures into adulthood.

The balance between tolerating a child on conditions that are imposed in order to guide, organize, and secure a workable home, and the unconditional hospitality that welcomes a child even when she is acting outside of the conditions of tolerance is difficult to find and maintain. Tolerance and unconditional hospitality tug at a parent's gut, as does the choice to offer conditional and unconditional forgiveness. On the one hand, parents have a responsibility to check children, to reprimand and punish them in response to wrongful behavior. Conditional forgiveness is contingent on the punishment being served. A teenager's free time with friends after school might be denied until a room is cleaned, a toddler's rudeness to others will be forgiven only after time alone in his room, and funds to an alcoholic family member may be cut off until she seeks out the help she needs. These are difficult, sometimes gut-wrenching, decisions that parents must make. But without reasonable conditions that are steadfastly enforced, civility will escape family life.

But to persevere as an effective parent, capable of joy and wholesome love, which are essential to the healthy development of children, we need to remain open to unconditional forgiveness. As difficult as it sometimes is, on some level, we accept our children as they are, in their incomprehensible difference from us and from what we expect. As the New Testament teaches us, it is the prodigal son that is most welcome at the dinner table, the one over whom the biggest fuss is made. To his sibling, there is no valid explanation for this fuss. In fact, to him it seems unfair. But the father remains open to the return of his wayward son and welcomes him home without any terms or conditions.

Unconditional forgiveness and unconditional hospitality are acts of faith. They are offered without justification and without merit. In offering these gifts to children, parents assume the risk inherent in any act of faith. It is a relinquishment of control and an acknowledgment that we are at the mercy of the hidden dimensions of our children's lives, which we do not fully comprehend. In remaining open to behaviors, attitudes, and decisions that go beyond or even conflict with our expectations, we risk condoning what ought to be reprimanded.

On the other hand, by trying to retain too much control, we risk stifling what needs to be left alone and free in a child's personality. Whether intervening with conditions and terms, or letting the child be, we are called to walk a fine line between the seen and unseen, the known and the unknowable, the conditional and the unconditional. And each time we choose one of the two, we risk our credibility and our effectiveness as parents. Yet we must choose. And as Kierkegaard reminds us, the meaning of our lives will be determined in large part by the seriousness with which we approach these choices. The choices we make become the life we choose. For parents, the choices we make also become, in part, the lives our children will lead. Most often, our choices are made with only a partial view of the situation, incomplete knowledge of the relevant data. We choose with intensity, but we choose also with faith: faith in our children and the incomprehensible potential and resilience that resides beneath their laughs and tears, successes and failures, joys and pains.

THE DOUBLE REGISTER

To have faith in a child is to remain open to and repeatedly affirm the unknowable, the unpredictable, and the irrational. At the same time that we work at meeting our obligation to be reasonable, to set limits and conditions by which children can live and learn, we are also required to accept and affirm what is beyond the reasonable. When they reject our advice and deny our requests, we can disagree and sometimes have an obligation to admonish, but we carry on with our affirmation of their lives. We feel disappointment, even anger, when they refuse to hear sound advice, but we retain our hope and our faith in them and their future. We remain open to their points of view and try to learn from their decisions, as well as our own, because we know that we do not have all of the answers to the questions of our own lives, much less of theirs. We know that what motivates and drives them is often beyond our comprehension. We listen, watch, and interpret, searching for the sense and the meaning in what they do. In fulfilling our obligation to provide conditions and limits in order to help our children develop healthy habits for living, we remain open to the unpredictable and often irrational forces of their inner lives and their future without conditions. This openness is a parent's faith in the child. And this faith protects us and our relationships with our children from being reduced to contentious power struggles and disheartening disagreements. This faith provides us with the psychological space to step back from our disagreements with their actions, decisions, and motivations. This space makes it possible for us to find new and creative ways of helping them to find their own way, their own voice, and their own principles for living. It enables us to help them accept the hidden dimensions of their own lives and to have faith in themselves and in us.

Finding and preserving the balance between the conditional and the unconditional, the seen and the unseen, is an art form that is very difficult to master. The right action or decision is rarely the obvious or the easy one. Faith involves risk, and to take risks we need courage. The courage to take risks is tied to the hope that the risk is worthwhile. Jumping off a bridge with a bungee cord tied around one's waist is a risk, but for the thrill-seeker it is worth it. Investing money in an unproven venture is worth the risk to the capitalist. To believe in a God without any hard evidence of his existence is to risk the meaning of one's life. But the promise of salvation is worth it to the theist.

Philosophical faith also involves risk and courage. It takes courage to believe in a child that is overly defiant or recklessly disrespectful. Only a faithful parent will engage in the difficult work required to bring a teenager back from the claws of substance addiction. It takes faith and courage to believe in one's ideas when they are at odds with the communities in which we live. But the parent that reverses the practices that send confusing messages to children at sporting events will not only be doing her children and her community a great service; she will also find great personal fulfillment by honoring her higher self.

To believe in oneself, in one's genius, is a risk because we could be wrong. But as parents, we really have little choice. The social mores that permeate the lives of our children require us to offer something different. We can only do this by turning inward to our higher selves and by turning a steady, rational gaze upon the world and our children to uncover their hidden depths and potential. It is out of these over-looked dimensions of our own lives and the lives of our children that the unique character of our lives is forged. To ignore these dimensions is to abandon the innate potential for greatness that every human being has. With philosophical faith, we will uncover this potential and enjoy the fulfillment of a life that strives for greatness.

EPILOGUE

Turning Inward

Parents face enormous challenges in raising children today. Given the daily grind of getting kids to school, getting to work on time, helping with homework, providing transportation to activities, comforting hurt feelings and bodies, and paying bills, all of which is carried out in an atmosphere of economic uncertainty, war, and environmental breakdown, it is no mystery as to why our days are filled with anxiety. In such a climate, it might seem unrealistic to expect parents to initiate processes of change in pursuit of greater fulfillment in their lives and the lives of their families. And yet the seven turning points of power, advocacy, guilt, community, gratitude, forgiveness, and faith demonstrate that even under the most difficult circumstances, parental change and fulfillment are possible.

It is at these turning points that parents either turn away from or overcome the double-sided challenge to responsibly raise well-adjusted children while also finding real and sustainable fulfillment in our own lives. For many parents, the routines of daily life seem overwhelming and leave us feeling as if there is no way to make things better. We simply struggle to make it through each day and regard those who seem to have it easier with envy. This mind-set, so common among parents today, might be the most difficult obstacle to overcome in making real, meaningful change in how we parent because this mind-set does not believe change is possible, in which case it isn't. This lack of belief, which is equivalent to a lack of hope, leaves parents feeling trapped. We imprison ourselves simply by failing to believe in the power we have to make changes.

FAITH AND FREEDOM

Tillich describes faith as a matter of freedom, which is "nothing more than the possibility of centered personal acts."[1] The free individual is one who plays an active role in directing his life. The obstacles to choosing what he wants to do with his life, whether those obstacles are self-doubt, incomplete understanding, or emotional turmoil, do not overwhelm one who executes centered personal acts. A person who is centered knows what he wants to do and why he wants to do it. He remains focused on his goal, even if he does not fully understand what it takes to achieve it or what its consequences will be. Life does not direct him; he directs his life.

Without a clear sense of direction, values, and goals, however, it is easy to lose sight of what we are trying to accomplish as parents. It often feels as if we are moving so quickly, we can only see the obstacles that are immediately in front of us and fail to see the general direction in which we are traveling. After a while, we look up to see that we have arrived far away from where had expected to be. Along the way we don't recognize that we are moving off course because it seems as if we are freely directing our lives in response to the world. We express our points of view in conversations, but fail to recognize that the conversations in which we participate have already determined what we will talk about. They provide the context for what can be meaningfully expressed, and once we are in it, it is often too late when we recognize that a particular conversation has pulled us away from our values and goals. We tend to deceive ourselves into thinking that we are forging our own path by engaging in the give and take of each day, when in reality we are progressing like two people on the subway who are so preoccupied with each other that they fail to realize they are on the wrong train. Parents can avoid taking the wrong path by reflecting on habits of thinking and acting as well as on the conversations, activities, and friends we engage. If we do not, we are likely to be carried away from our true values and goals by the tide of social acceptance.

Being pulled off course is a very real danger for parents who are faced with so many pressures to move in different directions. Insofar as we succumb to these pressures blindly, we diminish our ability to direct our lives and to adequately guide our children. Children look to us for direction, even if their incessant demands and tirades say otherwise. To provide that direction, we need to know where we want to lead them, what values we want them to live by, and which ideals we want them to aspire to. To do this, we must first believe in our values and goals and we must believe that it is worthwhile to resist the trends, expectations, and comforts that conflict with our goals and values. Parents may know the value of cooking healthy food and sharing dinner as a family, but the pace of everyday life makes the convenience of take-out too alluring to resist. Instead of a time to share food and stories, dinnertime becomes an exercise in expediency and pulls us away from time with family to share stories, concerns, and issues that matter.

Because the habits and patterns of daily life are familiar, it is often easier to accept them as our fate, as our only possibility, than it is to change them. In fact, we often see better alternatives to the way we are raising our children, but as long as we do not firmly believe in these alternatives we will not make the commitment and effort required to make them become a part of our lives. To adopt an alternative way of relating to others, especially our children, we need to change deeply entrenched habits of thinking and acting. Such change requires sacrifice, and sacrifice involves hardship. We will endure this difficulty only if we are convinced that the alternatives we are pursuing are worthwhile. Without this conviction, we will continue to look at the alternatives like a spectator who watches the game but never plays. For those with an inadequate belief in themselves and in the worthiness of change, alternative styles of parenting become something for others to pursue. Without the belief that alternatives are possible and worth pursuing, parents will never look beyond the habits by which they already live. A prerequisite to overcoming obstacles such as self-doubt, misunderstood emotions, or social expectations is the belief that it is possible to do so. Without this belief, we abandon our freedom and the possibility for change.

MAKING CHANGE HAPPEN

The characters we met in the seven turning points acted on faith—faith in themselves and in their freedom to abide by values central to who they are. In doing so, they were able to accomplish change in many different ways, some dramatic and some subtle. Jim and Jen, for instance, decided to leave the life they built as highly successful professionals in New York City to undertake a completely different lifestyle in the country. This was a rather dramatic change in response to the special needs of their son, Dennis, and it led them to discover a deep sense of gratitude, a dimension to life that was completely absent in the city. In contrast, Will Bookman did not have to move anywhere to work through his guilt, one of the more stubborn turning points that parents face. Without leaving his study, he examined the way he responded to his daughter's failure to meet his expectations of her. He discovered that his reaction had accomplished the exact opposite of what he set out to do, which was to help his daughter study for her exams. His guilt forced him to look within himself in order to find a different, more effective approach with his daughter. So whether we change professions, geography, or never leave our desk, real change is possible because it occurs within ourselves.

Perhaps the most emotionally charged turning point of the seven is forgiveness. The Amish community of Lancaster, Pennsylvania, demonstrated an almost superhuman capacity to forgive. Their gestures of forgiveness and compassion toward the family of the man who murdered their children in the immediate aftermath of the tragedy seem almost impossible for the rest of us, and it probably is. Forgiveness was possible, almost natural, for the Amish because it has been a cornerstone of their community and their culture for centuries and it is reinforced in their prayers and rituals every day. When tragedy struck, they turned to what they knew and trusted in, which is the virtue of forgiveness.

This story has at least two important lessons for parents as we consider making real changes in our lives. First, in times of crises and stress, we almost always rely on what is most familiar to us. We revert to behavior that is deeply ingrained in our personalities. Jim Healy, for example, attempted to transfer his power and strength as a worker to his role as a father. The use of force was familiar to him, so when his son rebelled, he used his authority and strength to clamp down hard on him. A lawyer whose son loses his starting spot on his high school basketball team tries to overrun the coach's decision by bringing his case to the athletic director. In doing so, he is reverting to what is familiar and to what he is good at. In the process, however, he fails to recognize that he is not helping his son by getting him favors he hasn't earned. Bert Maroney helped him to realize that he could benefit his son, and expand his own horizon of possibilities as an adult, by letting his son work through the disappointment on his own.

Making real and lasting change is difficult for most adults. Some can make changes spontaneously such as a person who drinks for years and suddenly decides that he has had enough and throws away the bottle for good. The overweight person wakes up one day and says to himself, "This is not who I want to be," and begins a life of exercise and healthy eating. For families, however, this method of change rarely works because families are made up of more than individuals. To ensure real and lasting change, change that will survive the obstacles and battles of household life, we need to cultivate the habits we desire step by step. Change in families, then, is best instituted in small increments that build on each other. Using the Amish as a model, successful change will occur if the behaviors we desire become the habits we live by. They become habits by building them into our daily routines. This is what Jim and Jen found themselves doing in saying grace before each meal when they moved to the country, reinforcing their sense of gratitude for their son and for the new life he led them to discover.

Many parents know that the most effective way to accomplish change in family life is to work in small increments. And while this approach may be necessary, it is rarely sufficient to sustain the habits we want to live by. The practice of building habits by small increments needs to be supplemented with the second lesson of the Amish story—the need for a well-defined worldview.

For the Amish, forgiveness is a part of their daily lives because it is grounded in their understanding of the world as Christians. Their Christian faith teaches them that their lives depend on God. The purpose of their existence is to serve God, and their greatest hope is to achieve salvation through God's mercy. In order to have a chance of realizing this hope, they need God's forgiveness. The only way they can earn God's forgiveness is by offering their own forgiveness to others. By having such a clear worldview and such a clear understanding of their place in that world, the Amish are able to sustain their commitment to forgiveness under the absolute worst circumstances. The habits they live by are powerful because they make sense to them in the context of their world. Even if we do not share their worldview, we can learn a great deal from the role it plays in Amish life.

The good news is that we all have a worldview, whether or not we are aware of it. That is, we all have a set of priorities, principles, and values by which we live. For most of us, however, this worldview, and the values that constitute it, are not very clear to us. As a result, we find ourselves unsure of what we value most, and this uncertainty leads us to hold or pursue conflicting goods. A father, for instance, wants his children to eat well, but he is rushing out the door to play a basketball game at dinner time. At that moment, he is making his exercise a priority. This does not make him a terrible person; it simply indicates his priorities at that moment. He wants his children to eat well and he wants to exercise. Given the time constraints of his life, he must choose between them. If he is dissatisfied with having to choose, he may examine his schedule more carefully and try to maintain both goods—his exercise and time to ensure that his children have a healthy dinner. In order to uphold both of these priorities at the same time, he may have to make time by eliminating another activity from his day. In order to make these changes, however, he must clarify his priorities and what he values most.

It may turn out that his responsibilities do not allow him to free up more time earlier in the day. This will force him to either find a more innovative way to accommodate both his children and himself, or he will have to choose one over the other. Parents make these choices regularly. In doing so, we express who we are. That is, our choices tell us what is most important to us. If we are clear about the worldview by which and in which we want to live, we will discover that it supports our choices and gives us confidence that our choices are the right ones. The clarity of their worldview and how they fit into it accounts for much of the strength of the Amish. This clarity is what we need if we are to sustain the small, incremental changes necessary in working through parental turning points.

FINDING A WORLDVIEW

The decline of religion in the modern world has left many without a clear sense of their place in the world. We find ourselves faced with many competing goods and, as a result, we are often uncertain and confused about where we are, where we're going, and where we're leading our children. The Amish example makes clear the benefits of a clear worldview, but for those of us who lack one, where do we look to find it? Again, the seven turning points indicate that the answer is within.

Philosophy is not only a process of remembering; it is also a process of listening. The problem for parents is that we spend most of our time listening to others, in particular, our children. In order to identify the steel beams, the goods that will support the construction of an enduring worldview, we need to first find the time and the will to listen to ourselves. We already have the components of our own worldview inside of ourselves. The goods that we pursue each day are a clear indication of the worldview we hold and the things we value most. By paying careful attention to them, we can see if our habits express the type of character we want to have. If we are to elevate these goods and values into a coherent worldview, we need to hear what they are saying to us and about us.

The inner self is always sending messages to us about our own lives through our thoughts, emotions, and feelings. If the emotions that dominate our lives are negative—jealously, anger, resentment, hate—it is a clear sign that we are not happy with the direction of our lives. Negative emotions indicate that we are out of step with ourselves and we need to change. If we are lethargic or find ourselves binging on junk food, turning our bodies into doughy garbage bins, it is a good indication that we are seeking short-term satisfaction over long-term fulfillment. Such short-term satisfaction is usually sought because we feel trapped, as if there is no way to achieve long-term fulfillment or the effort required is not worth it. This behavior is an indication that we have given up on the possibility of becoming more or better than we already are. The fire of our lives has been dimmed and we have gotten used to it. Rather than trying to lift the shade from our window to let the sunlight in, we turn on a sixty-watt bulb and make believe that is all the light there is.

Or, to switch metaphors, when we find ourselves confronted with conflicting goods or conflicting emotions, we are hearing sound bites of information about ourselves when a detailed narrative is required. Conflicting goods and emotions are like muffled sounds squeezing through a door, the echo of the real interests, values, and passions of our innermost self. In order to be who we want to be and go where we want to go in life, we need to open that door to clearly hear what the hidden and neglected inner parts of the self are telling us. This is what Will Bookman and his coworker, Steve Shannon, did by listening to their consciences when they felt the pang of guilt that arose in their relationships with their daughters. It is what Jim Hartly did on the porch of his daughter's music school when he listened to the voices of quiet communities from the past that reignited his commitment to the values he held most deeply. This quiet listening enabled him to overcome self-doubt about his career, his effectiveness as a father and husband, and the place of his family in his community.

CULTIVATING LISTENING SKILL

Listening is more than a biological or physiological function. It is a skill that requires practice if one is to do it well. In our fast-paced world, most of us do not have the time to concentrate on how well we listen to others or ourselves. This is unfortunate, because in hearing others well, we connect with them deeply. This connection can be the source of great joy.

The ability to listen is also a good indication of how well-developed we are as people. Poor listeners are stuck at the level of the ego-self. They see the other in a conversation as someone to be spoken to, but not heard. The poor listener waits for his opportunity to interject his thoughts, unconcerned with what the other has to say. For children, it can be devastating to have a poor listener as a parent. To go through one's childhood misunderstood or ignored by a parent who is compelled to control conversations and who cannot or will not hear what his child is trying to say is painful and destructive to a child.

A parent who cannot listen to a child usually cannot listen to himself, either. And just as a parent's poor listening is destructive to a child's development, it is also destructive to his own development. In not listening to our inner selves, in not hearing our deepest concerns, we cannot know what we truly value, nor can we have a clear worldview. In not knowing the goods that are most in tune with who we want to be, we end up being tossed and turned by whatever social wind is blowing at the time. Our goods conflict and we feel stuck in our development. We get caught in a rut because we have no clear direction of where we want to go or where we want to lead our families. So we can benefit our children and ourselves by taking the time we need to find out what goods resonate with us most deeply. These goods will form the structure of our worldview and provide the direction we need to live a fulfilling life.

This is what we can accomplish by working through turning points in our lives. We have the resources within ourselves to do this work. If we reflect on these internal resources and hear what they tell us about who we want to be and how we want to live, we will find the autonomy and strength we need to find real fulfillment in our lives as parents. We will discover that growing up is not only for children, but also for us. And to accept this challenge by working through turning points as they arise, we live better lives and become better parents.

NOTES

INTRODUCTION: PHILOSOPHY AND STORY

1. Richard Kearney, *On Stories* (New York: Routledge, 2006).
2. Kearney, *On Stories*, 6.

1. POWER

1. Ralph Waldo Emerson, *Selected Essays* (New York: Penguin Books, 1984), 55.
2. Baruch Spinoza, *The Ethics and Selected Letters* (Indianapolis: Hackett Books, 1982).
3. Spinoza, *The Ethics*, 75.

2. ADVOCACY

1. Emmanuel Levinas, *Totality and Infinity: An Essay on Exteriority*, trans. Alphonso Lingis (Pittsburgh: Duquesne University Press, 1969).
2. Plato, *Great Dialogues of Plato*, ed. Eric Warmington and Philip Rouse (New York: Mentor Books, 1984).

3. Ralph Waldo Emerson, *Selected Essays* (New York: Penguin Books, 1984).

3. GUILT

1. Irvin Yalom, *Existential Psychotherapy* (New York: Basic Books, 1980).
2. Martin Heidegger, *Being and Time*, trans. John MacQuarrie and Edward Robinson (New York: Harper Collins, 1962).

4. COMMUNITY

1. Ralph Waldo Emerson, *Selected Essays* (New York: Penguin Books, 1984), 181.
2. Emerson, *Selected Essays*, 176.
3. Emerson, *Selected Essays*, 178.
4. Emerson, *Selected Essays*, 176.
5. Alice Miller, *The Drama of the Gifted Child: The Search for the True Self* (New York: Perseus, 1997).

5. GRATITUDE

1. Baruch Spinoza, *The Ethics and Selected Letters* (Indianapolis: Hackett Books, 1982), 149.

6. FORGIVENESS

1. Simon Wiesenthal, *The Sunflower: On the Possibilities and Limits of Forgiveness* (New York: Schocken Books, 1998).
2. Donald Kraybill, Stephen Nolt, and David Weaver Zorchor, *Amish Grace: How Forgiveness Transcended Tragedy* (San Francisco: Jossey-Bass, 2007).
3. Andre Compte-Spoonville, *A Small Treatise on the Great Virtues: The Uses of Philosophy in Everyday Life* (New York: Metropolitan, 2001).
4. Compte-Spoonville, *A Small Treatise*, 155.
5. Henry Wansbrough, ed., *The New Jerusalem Bible* (New York: Doubleday, 1990).

6. Oscar Wilde, *The Picture of Dorian Gray* (New York: W. W. Norton, 2006).

7. Leo Tolstoy, *The Death of Ivan Ilych and Other Stories*, trans. Alymer Maude (New York: Signet, 1976).

7. FAITH

1. Seamus Carey, *The Faithful Parent: Discovering the Spirit of Purposeful Parenting* (Lanham, MD: Rowman and Littlefield, 2007).

2. Ralph Waldo Emerson, *Selected Essays* (New York: Penguin Books, 1984), 176.

3. Emerson, *Selected Essays*, 178.

4. Robert McKirahan, *Philosophy Before Socrates: An Introduction with Text and Commentary* (Indianapolis: Hackett Books, 1994).

5. Friedrich Nietzsche, *Philosophy in the Tragic Age of the Greeks*, trans. Marianne Cowan (Washington, DC: Regnery Publishing, 1998), 56.

6. Paul Tillich, *The Dynamics of Faith* (New York: Harper and Row, 1957), 16.

7. Tillich, *The Dynamics*, 5.

EPILOGUE: TURNING INWARD

1. Paul Tillich, *The Dynamics of Faith* (New York: Harper and Row, 1957), 5.

BIBLIOGRAPHY

Aristotle. *Introduction to Aristotle*. Edited by Richard McKeon. New York: Random House, 1947.

Borradori, Giovanna. *Philosophy in an Age of Terror: Dialogues with Jurgen Habermas and Jacques Derrida*. Chicago: University of Chicago Press, 2003.

Boyer, Ernest, Jr. *A Way in the World: Family Life as Spiritual Discipline*. San Francisco: Harper and Row, 1984.

Caputo, John. *The Prayers and Tears of Jacques Derrida: Religion without Religion*. Bloomington: Indiana University Press, 1997.

———. *Radical Hermeneutics: Repetition, Deconstruction, and the Hermeneutic Project*. Bloomington: Indiana University Press, 1987.

Carey, Seamus. *The Faithful Parent: Discovering the Sprit of Purposeful Parenting*. Lanham, MD: Rowman and Littlefield, 2007.

———. *The Whole Child: Restoring Wonder to the Art of Parenting*. Lanham, MD: Rowman and Littlefield, 2003.

Coles, Robert. *The Moral Intelligence of Children: How to Raise a Moral Child*. New York: Random House, 1997.

Commission on Children at Risk. *Hardwired to Connect: The New Scientific Case for Authoritative Communities*. New York: Institute for American Values, 2003.

Compte-Spoonville, Andre. *A Small Treatise on the Great Virtues: The Uses of Philosophy in Everyday Life*. New York: Metropolitan, 2001.

Emerson, Ralph Waldo. *Selected Essays*. New York: Penguin Books, 1984.

Erikson, Eric. *Identity and the Life Cycle*. New York: W. W. Norton and Company, 1980.

Galinsky, Ellen. *Ask the Children: The Breakthrough Study that Reveals How to Succeed at Work and Parenting*. New York: Harper Collins, 1999.

———. *The Six Stages of Parenthood*. Cambridge: Perseus Books, 1987.

Ginzburg, Natalia. *The Little Virtues*. Translated by Dick Davis. Manchester: Carcanet Press, 1985.

Heidegger, Martin. *Basic Writings*. Translated by David Farrell Krell. San Francisco: Harper Collins, 1993.

———. *Being and Time*. Translated by John Macquarrie and Edward Robinson. New York: Harper Collins, 1962.

Jankelevitech, Vladimir. *Forgiveness*. Translated by Andrew Kelly. Chicago: University of Chicago Press, 2005.

Kearney, Richard. *On Stories*. New York: Routledge, 2006.

———. *Strangers, Gods and Monsters*. New York: Routledge, 2003.

Kierkegaard, Søren. *Fear and Trembling*. Translated and edited by Howard V. Hong and Edna H. Hong. Princeton, NJ: Princeton University Press, 1983.

Kindlon, Dan, and Michael Thompson. *Raising Cain: Protecting the Emotional Life of Boys*. New York: Ballentine Books, 2000.

Kraybill, Donald, Steven Nolt, and David Weaver Zorchor. *Amish Grace: How Forgiveness Transcended Tragedy*. San Francisco: Jossey-Bass, 2007.

Levin, David Michael. *The Listening Self: Personal Growth, Social Change, and the Closure of Metaphysics*. New York: Routledge, 1989.

———. *The Philosopher's Gaze: Modernity in the Shadows of Enlightenment*. California: University of California Press, 1999.

Levinas, Emmanuel. *Totality and Infinity: An Essay on Exteriority*. Translated by Alphonso Lingis. Pittsburgh: Duquesne University Press, 1969.

McKirahan, Robert. *Philosophy Before Socrates: An Introduction with Text and Commentary*. Indianapolis: Hackett Books, 1994.

Merleau-Ponty, Maurice. *The Visible and the Invisible*. Evanston, IL: Northwestern University Press, 1968.

Miller, Alice. *The Drama of the Gifted Child: The Search for the True Self*. New York: Perseus, 1997.

Neitzsche, Friedrich. *Philosophy in the Tragic Age of the Greeks*. Translated by Marianne Cowan. Washington, DC: Regnery Publishing, 1998.

Plato. *Great Dialogues of Plato*. Edited by Eric Warmington and Philip Rouse. New York: Mentor Books, 1984.

Putnam, Robert. *Bowling Alone: The Collapse and Revival of American Community*. New York: Simon and Schuster, 2000.

Simmons, Rachel. *Odd Girl Out: The Hidden Aggression in Girls*. New York: Harcourt Books, 2003.

Smith, Steven. *Spinoza's Book of Life: Freedom and Redemption in the Ethics*. New Haven, CT: Yale University Press, 2003.

Spinoza, Baruch. *The Ethics and Selected Letters*. Indianapolis: Hackett Books, 1982.

Taylor, Charles. *Sources of the Self: The Making of the Modern Identity*. Cambridge, MA: Harvard University Press, 1989.

Tillich, Paul. *The Courage to Be*. New Haven, CT: Yale University Press, 1952.

———. *The Dynamics of Faith*. New York: Harper and Row, 1957.

Tolstoy, Leo. *The Death of Ivan Ilych and Other Stories*. Translated by Alymer Maude. New York: Signet, 1976.

Wansbrough, Henry, ed. *The New Jerusalem Bible*. New York: Doubleday, 1990.

Westphal, Merold. *God, Guilt, and Death: An Existential Phenomenology of Religion*. Bloomington: Indiana University Press, 1984.

———. *Transcendence and Self-Transcendence*. Bloomington: Indiana University Press, 2004.

Wiesenthal, Simon. *The Sunflower: On the Possibilities and Limits of Forgiveness*. New York: Schocken Books, 1998.

Wilde, Oscar. *Picture of Dorian Gray*. New York: W. W. Norton, 2006.

Yalom, Irvin. *Existential Psychotherapy*. New York: Basic Books, 1980.

INDEX

ABOUT THE AUTHOR

Seamus Carey is professor and chair of the Philosophy Department at Manhattan College in Riverdale, New York. He is the author of *The Whole Child: Restoring Wonder to the Art of Parenting* (2003) and *The Faithful Parent: Discovering the Spirit of Purposeful Parenting* (2007). Dr. Carey lives in Pelham Manor, New York, with his wife and three children.